# PAPA'S BLESSINGS

## The Gift That Keeps Giving

DR. GREG BOURGOND

iUniverse, Inc.
Bloomington

Papa's Blessings
The Gift That Keeps Giving

iUniverse books may be ordered through booksellers or by contacting:

iUniverse
1663 Liberty Drive
Bloomington, IN 47403
www.iuniverse.com
1-800-Authors (1-800-288-4677)

ISBN: 978-1-4620-0335-8 (sc)
ISBN: 978-1-4620-0336-5 (hc)
ISBN: 978-1-4620-0337-2 (e)

Library of Congress Control Number: 2011909648

Printed in the United States of America

iUniverse rev. date: 6/24/2011

This book is dedicated to Chad and Monique, loving father and mother to our grandchildren Derrick, Braedan, Talisa, Kieran, Gaelan, and Lochlan, and to my mother, Violette, who was a repeated blessing in my life, imparting grace, mercy, and unconditional love in large doses at regular intervals throughout her life.

# Contents

Foreword . . . . . . . . . . . . . . . . . .ix

Preface. . . . . . . . . . . . . . . . . . .xi

Acknowledgments. . . . . . . . . . . . . xv

Introduction. . . . . . . . . . . . . . . .xvii

CHAPTER 1    The Importance of Blessing . . 1

CHAPTER 2    The Source of Blessing. . . . . 8

CHAPTER 3    The Power of Blessing . . . . 20

CHAPTER 4    The Essentials of Blessing . . 30

CHAPTER 5    The Preparation of Blessing . 44

CHAPTER 6    The Realization of Blessing . 69

CHAPTER 7    The Legacy of Blessing. . . . 77

APPENDIX A   Bibliography. . . . . . . . . 89

APPENDIX B   The Blessing Worksheet . . . 91

APPENDIX C   About the Author . . . . . . 97

APPENDIX D   Previous Work. . . . . . . . .101

# Foreword

*Papa's Blessing* by Greg Bourgond

Foreword by Robert V. Rakestraw

February 1, 2011

This is an important book and a practical book. It is important because it addresses a great—one could even say desperate—need in our society for many young, middle-aged, and, in some cases, older persons to experience blessings from those they look up to, especially their parents, grandparents, and others in some sense responsible for their care and well-being. This is also a practical book because of the fine job the author has done of explaining the what, the why, and the how of giving a blessing to someone.

A blessing is understood as an act of declaring or wishing God's favor and goodness upon someone. It is not only a wish but a purposeful declaration of God's intentions for the person, much like a benediction. Dr. Bourgond lays a solid scriptural foundation for the practice of blessing, and then he presents illuminating examples of blessing from the Bible and from his family life and extensive ministry of blessing.

Readers will appreciate Greg's resolute yet gentle approach to the practice of blessing, rather than for a dogmatic set of prescriptions. Those who prefer may modify certain suggestions in the book according to their own preferences, as God leads. The author's desire is not to lay out a set of rules but to give fathers, mothers, grandparents, and others the information and motivation for blessing those under their care and influence.

Because of this book's biblical character, and because of the chronic and widespread failure of parents and other responsible people to affirm verbally their children and others in need, I recommend this book to any and all who desire to be a living blessing and permanent benediction to many throughout their lives.

Robert V. Rakestraw
Professor of Theology Emeritus
Bethel Theological Seminary

# PREFACE

Formally blessing our loved ones or others within our sphere of influence is a relatively rare occurrence today. Yet, wherever I go to speak and the issue of blessing is addressed I find a longing thirst to receive a blessing or a deep sense of felt need to give a blessing to those who matter most in our lives. Regardless of nation, ethnicity, or culture the subject of blessing strikes an emotional chord in almost every person I meet along the way.

As president and founder of Heart of a Warrior Ministries, I have many opportunities to talk to young and old men alike. Most have never received a blessing from the people who mean the most to them, often their fathers. Yet, all long for a blessing from someone who matters to them. Men and women, boys and girls, need to be acknowledged, affirmed, appreciated, valued, and encouraged. Too often words of esteem, respect, and honor go unsaid.

When I speak to men and women about blessing, I witness an emotional response. Either a man or woman has received a blessing from someone of significance in their life, perhaps a father or a mother, a grandfather or a grandmother, an uncle or an aunt, or possibly a mentor, colleague, work associate, pastor, or close friend, or they have not. Those that haven't, long for the experience and those that have, cherish the memory.

The world can be a cold, dark, and dangerous place. In *After Virtue: A Study in Moral Theory*, Alasdair MacIntyre, senior research professor of philosophy at the University of Notre Dame, commented on our culture today by comparing it to the Dark Ages. He makes the following comment: "A crucial turning point in that earlier history occurred when men and women of good will turned aside from the task of shoring up the Roman imperium and ceased to identify the continuation of civility and moral community with the maintenance of the imperium. What they set themselves to achieve instead—often not recognizing fully what they were doing—was the construction of new forms of community within which the moral life could be sustained so that both morality and civility might survive the coming ages of barbarism and darkness. If my account of our moral condition is correct, we ought also to conclude that for some time now we too have reached that turning point."

MacIntyre went on to say, "What matters at this stage is the construction of local forms of community within which civility and the intellectual and moral life can be sustained through the new dark ages which are already upon us. And if the tradition of the virtues was able to survive the horrors of the last dark ages, we are not entirely without ground for hope. This time, however, the barbarians are not waiting beyond the frontiers; they have already been governing us for quite some time. And it is our lack of consciousness of this that constitutes part of our predicament."[1]

The old dark ages were marked by fear of the unknown and reliance upon the learned for interpreting the world around them. Knowledge and wisdom resided with the aristocracy and the church. Individual study of God's word was left to the so-called scholars with agendas. Interpretation lay under the sole purview of these authorities. The common man and woman relied upon others for truth. The Reformation broke that bondage. Martin Luther's rebellion essentially gave the scriptures back to the people.

MacIntyre suggests we are in a new dark age. Living in the fast lane and susceptible to the tyranny of the urgent has compelled many of us to rely on new authorities for knowledge and wisdom. These subject matter experts can be found on newscasts, talk shows, newsstands, and some pulpits. Because of our hectic lifestyles, we turn to "sound bites" from popular celebrities inside and outside the church for "truth."

I agree with MacIntyre—we are living in the new dark ages.

---

1    Alasdair MacIntyre, *After Virtue: A Study in Moral Theory*, 3rd ed. (Notre Dame: Notre Dame Press, 2007), 263.

When the organizing center of our beliefs, values, worldview, and motives shifts from the Bible to a pluralistic syncretism and amalgamation of philosophies and ideologies, we are not far from losing our way and falling into factions and special interest groups fitting our preconceived notions and whims.

Regardless of your view of our current age, we can all agree to the need to help our loved ones navigate the world around them. One powerful way to do that is by blessing them with a blessing of hope for their future based on the foundation of God's word and the framework that recognizes their unique characteristics and potential. Whether they are a child or an adult, a blessing is a gift to them and for them, something they will look back on repeatedly when faced with adversity and difficulty, when needing guidance and direction, and when they need to be reminded that someone of importance in their life cares deeply for them and saw something of value in them.

I have received an overwhelming response in a variety of settings where the importance of blessing was addressed or where I had the opportunity to bless others. Many have asked how I selected values for my grandchildren or how I developed blessings for them. Still others have asked how they could do the same for people who mean the most to them, whether child or adult, son or daughter, father or mother, grandparent or relative, and so on.

I am deeply indebted to the significant body of work on blessing from Drs. John Trent, president and founder of StrongFamilies.com, committed to strengthening marriage and family relationships, and Gary Smalley, an expert on family relationships and interpersonal dynamics. I wholeheartedly recommend their book, *The Blessing: Giving the Gift of Unconditional Love and Acceptance.* I would also encourage the reader to visit the website www.TheBlessing.com.

This book will focus on the importance of blessing significant others who come within our circle of relationships. It will tell how to select values and develop blessings and will illustrate this work with examples. The book also outlines a process for drafting and administering a blessing. My perspectives on blessing are unapologetically influenced by my Christian faith and the Giver and Author of all blessing, our Creator and heavenly Father, God Almighty. I find it comforting referring to him as Abba, an Aramaic word found three times in the New Testament corresponding to our terms "Daddy" or "Papa."[2]

Dr. Greg Bourgond
Papa to my grandchildren on behalf of Abba—my Heavenly Father

---

2    Mark 14:36; Romans 8:15; Galatians 4:6.

# Acknowledgments

First and foremost I want to acknowledge the foundational work of Gary Smalley and John Trent. Their book, *The Blessing*, provided early inspiration to me. The blessings I wrote for my grandchildren early on were stimulated in part by the reading of their book. You may have heard it said there is nothing original. To some degree that is true. As authors we build on the foundations laid by others. As you read this book you will see their fingerprints.

Second, I want to acknowledge my daughter, son-in-law, and six grandchildren, who were the initial beneficiaries of blessings my wife and I were honored to administer in the wonderful setting of the White House at Green Lake Conference Center in Wisconsin. The blessings were originally written on a long plane ride home from Brazil when God laid it on my heart to do so. I still remember the tears that flowed as I wrote them.

Third, I want to acknowledge my mentor, Dr. J. Robert Clinton, former professor of leadership at Fuller Theological Seminary in Pasadena, California, who chose several of his mentorees, I being one of them, to receive a personal blessing from him. It was one of the most significant events in my life. I had given blessings to others but, up until that moment, had not received a blessing from anyone.

Fourth, I would like to acknowledge my wife of forty-two years, who not only gave me the platform I get to dance on but who also wrote and administered a blessing to me. Not many husbands receive a blessing from their wives. Debby has blessed me throughout my life with her unwavering love and support.

Fifth, I want to acknowledge my mother. She was a blessing to my brother, sisters, and me. There was never a moment I didn't feel her love, support, affirmation, approval, and esteem. She blessed me every time I spoke to her. Her memory is and will always be a blessing.

Finally, I want to acknowledge the many men over the years who I have had the privilege of blessing. Although I sought to bless them, they blessed me by allowing me to be an earthly surrogate for our heavenly Father. My life has been deeply enriched as a result.

# INTRODUCTION

As a young boy I longed for words of affirmation from my father. In my eyes he was a giant of a man, not in stature, but in life. As a self-made man he rose to the top of his field. He owned and operated an auto body repair shop, was a general manager of an automobile dealership, and in his retirement years was a cook on lake-going tugs. He was always good with his hands. He could turn a wreck into a work of art and a meal into a feast. He was my hero growing up. I knew he loved me and was proud of me. But I came to that realization listening to him talk about me to others. Rarely did I hear words of affirmation from him directly.

One incident comes to mind as I think about receiving the affirmation I sought from my father. When I was ten years old I joined a boxing team sponsored by the local police station. My dad was ecstatic. I was small for my age but made up for the lack of height by being fearless, tenacious, and persistent. My dad came to all my matches, cheered for me, and relished my hard-fought victories. He bought me a robe with my name on the back. It was a great time in our relationship. I felt his affirmation.

My boxing career came to an abrupt halt one day after my mother witnessed a fight I started with a neighbor kid. She became very worried and mad at the same time, declaring that boxing was corrupting her boy. She was always fearful I would be hurt. She was concerned when she saw me pick fights with boys much bigger than me. So, she unilaterally put an end to my budding boxing career. Her decision was a painful blow to me—this was the one place where I received the affirmation I so desperately wanted from my father.

Much of my early childhood was filled with a need for

approval from my father. But his relative absence in my life created a deep void. I remember the regular disappointments I experienced when he just wasn't around for me when I needed him the most. Yet, I deeply loved him and wanted to be like him. He was a man's man. I got my early cues about manhood from him. I mimicked him.

Our family life began to unravel with a growing rift between my father and mother. My older brother was in the navy at the time. My two younger sisters were at home with me. The arguments between my parents came with increasing frequency and became more heated and hurtful as time progressed. His drinking became a problem that fueled the arguments. I loved both my parents and hated the arguments between them.

I was in a Catholic parochial school during this tumultuous period and was lead altar boy for the local parish priest and regional bishop when he came to town. I felt the urge to serve God very early. Becoming a priest seemed my destiny. For me, catechism classes were exciting and opened my mind and heart to the majesty—and fear—of the Creator of the universe. One thing I learned from my Roman Catholic upbringing was a deep and awesome respect for the majesty of God. As a young boy I mistakenly believed that somehow I could mediate the turmoil and rancor by being a better boy, doing more than was expected of me, and appealing to God through acts of penance.

When an argument between my father and mother occurred I would employ two tactics. The first was to go to my bedroom and clean it. Somehow I thought doing so would mend the divide between my parents. This misplaced perspective was my feeble attempt at maintaining some control over the chaos in the home. By bringing order to my small world, I also thought somehow the heated confrontations would subside.

When things got particularly bad I would seek God's help. I remember vividly running to our church a few blocks away, bursting through the huge doors, making my way to the statue of Joseph, dropping to my knees, and pleading with God to bring healing to my home and stop the arguments. This self-made sanctuary was the only place I felt God's affirmation, His blessing. It was the only place where I experienced peace in my young life.

As the relationship between my father and mother deteriorated, I feared the worst. Having no reference for comparison in my small world, I conveniently thought this must be the norm for most families. After my father left the house to live elsewhere, my mother struggled to maintain her sanity in the midst of the tragedy of a failed marriage. My father found someone else to love. I looked for someone to blame. I felt abandoned. I felt rejected by the man that meant the most to me.

One terrible day I was called to the courthouse to declare with whom I preferred to live. As a twelve-year-old boy, I was confused and fearful. The judge was not sympathetic. He asked me to choose between two people I loved dearly. Not able to speak, the judge grew impatient. Finally, he leaned over the bench and said, "Hurry up son, we haven't got all day." I blurted out a response and ran from the courtroom. I chose my father and immediately felt that I betrayed my mother.

The emotions welled up in me as I pushed through the doors which led to cement steps outside the courthouse. On both sides of the steps were statues of lions. I remember throwing my arms around the neck of the lion on my right as I cried uncontrollably. I vowed I would never allow anyone to have that kind of control over my life again. I would never let anyone get that close to me again. That was the day my childhood ended.

My father quickly married his new love. My two sisters and I lived with them. His wife was a strict and uncompromising presence to be endured. Punishment was quick and severe. My dad turned our discipline over to her, which she meted out without mercy or grace. Appeals to him were met with deaf ears. I felt adrift, without any moorings. The blessing I longed for became a distant and fading dream.

When the toxic environment became unbearable for me, I ran away to join my mother, who had married an air force sergeant. I remember hiding under a bridge several miles from town but near where my mother and her new husband lived temporarily. I feared that my father or, worse yet, my stepmother would find me and drag me back to an unloving and uncaring place of torment. At least, that is how I viewed it at that time.

As time passed my stepfather became my surrogate father, who cared for me, watched over me, defended me, provided for me, and raised me as best he could. I still longed for the blessing of my natural father and made several attempts to reconnect with him. By then he was raising a new family, and his attentions were directed toward them. He offered little to no support. When I asked for financial assistance to attend college, he declined. His limited resources were directed to the needs of his new family.

I joined the navy and was married soon thereafter. My father-in-law was a model of virtue and faith lived out in bold relief. He respected and loved me. I felt his affirmation. I felt blessed to have him in my life. He died soon after Debby and I were married, just before the birth of our only daughter. Again, the man I admired and to whom I sought blessing was taken from me. My short exposure to him left a positive impact on my life, and he was one of the more significant contributing factors that led me to commit my life to Jesus Christ as my Lord and Savior.

After losing four babies prematurely, my wife gave birth to our only child, a baby girl born while I was heading home from Vietnam. When Debby became pregnant just before I left on a navy ship headed for the war zone, I shook my puny little fist in the face of God, thinking He would take this child too. Off the coast of Recife, Brazil, on our way home from the battlefront I received a message that our child was born. I was released from the ship while it was being refueled in Puerto Rico to fly to the bedside of my wife and newborn daughter.

Six months later, we were in Key West, Florida, where I attended a school on a new sonar system. My wife had dragged me to a Baptist church twice, where I heard the Gospel but did not believe I needed the message of God's redemption freely offered to me through the life, death, burial, and resurrection of His Son, Jesus Christ. My relationship with God up to that time was distant and remote. My experience of abandonment from my earthly father fueled a sense of abandonment from my heavenly Father.

One night I went into the room of my sleeping daughter. As I gazed upon her in the crib, I was overcome with emotion. I realized she was a blessing from God. We could not have any more children. Almost simultaneously, I also realized that Jesus was God's gift to me. The Gospel I had heard now made sense to me—that Jesus died for my sins and was God's provision for salvation and renewal of a personal relationship with Him. On August 11, 1973, I knelt before my daughter's crib and gave my heart, body, and soul to Jesus Christ and received his gift of grace and mercy. I had been truly blessed.

From that day to today I have felt the blessing of God in many ways through His involvement in my life and at the hands of many people who have blessed me with their presence, affirmation, support, and guidance. God filled the void I experienced in the past with His blessing. In retrospect, I can now see God's blessing at many junctures where He repeatedly met me at my time of need. I have come to realize how important a blessing is to all human beings.

Over the course of my life I repeatedly experienced firsthand the longing of others for a blessing—a seal of approval from those who matter most to us administered by meaningful touch, spoken word, placing value in the one being blessed, a picture of a preferable future, a commitment to seeing that future realized—all established, informed, conditioned, and energized by scripture.

Every man, woman, and child longs for a blessing from those who mean the most to them. Every son and daughter longs for the affirmation of those who hold significance in their life. I have had the opportunity to address many audiences nationally and internationally with messages underscoring the importance of a blessing from God and from those who we respect, those who are significant in our life, those who raised us, those who have had positive influence over us, those who have supported the pursuit of our dreams, those who have mentored us, those who have breathed life into us, those who have ministered to us, and those who have met our greatest needs along the journey we call life.

# Chapter 1
## *The Importance of Blessing*

THE IMPORTANCE OF pronouncing blessing in someone's life cannot be overstressed. Many of us have experienced the pain of negative remarks made about us. All too often they come from those who should have our best interest at heart. You may have heard that sticks and stones may break our bones but names will never harm us. That is not true. Debilitating pronouncements come in many forms: uncomplimentary statements, hurtful criticisms, unflattering gossip, biting sarcasm, negative insinuations, disparaging remarks, unfounded disapproval, condemnation, denunciation, personal denigration, vilification, defamation, belittlement, libel, and other verbally abusive comments.

People in general and children specifically absorb negative proclamations into the deepest recesses of their soul. Repeated often enough, they begin to formulate an unhealthy view of one's self. Those on the receiving end of this kind of verbal abuse often become in person what is said about them. They begin to believe that is who they really are. Their self-image is distorted and progressively destroyed, leading to dysfunctional or destructive lives. No wound is greater than one received from a parent.

Some of the greatest harm we do to our children is to label them with unhealthy, uncomplimentary, and damaging emotional assertions. "You're stupid." "You'll never amount to anything." "You're just like so and so." "You can't do anything

1

right." "You're an idiot." "You're a failure." Such quips are in fact a curse, even if you meant to stimulate needed change in the life of a loved one. It takes many more positive statements to overcome the effects of one negative statement. Our children become what we name them.

There is an old adage that says, "If you can't say something good about someone, don't say anything at all." The Bible talks about the power of the tongue for good or for bad.

> *Not many of you should presume to be teachers, my brothers, because you know that we who teach will be judged more strictly. We all stumble in many ways. If anyone is never at fault in what he says, he is a perfect man, able to keep his whole body in check. When we put bits into the mouths of horses to make them obey us, we can turn the whole animal. Or take ships as an example. Although they are so large and are driven by strong winds, they are steered by a very small rudder wherever the pilot wants to go. Likewise the tongue is a small part of the body, but it makes great boasts. Consider what a great forest is set on fire by a small spark. The tongue also is a fire, a world of evil among the parts of the body. It corrupts the whole person, sets the whole course of his life on fire, and is itself set on fire by hell. All kinds of animals, birds, reptiles, and creatures of the sea are being tamed and have been tamed by man, but no man can tame the tongue. It is a restless evil, full of deadly poison. With the tongue we praise our Lord and Father, and with it we curse men, who have been made in God's likeness. Out of the same mouth come praise and cursing. My brothers, this should not be. Can both fresh water and salt water flow from the same spring? My brothers, can a fig tree bear olives, or a grapevine bear figs? Neither can a salt spring produce fresh water.* **James 3:1–12 NIV**

## A Story of Blessing

Last May, I was at a retreat center in Pine Valley, California. I had been asked to speak to a gathering of men from several churches in the area. My second message to them was preceded by a video clip from the movie *Gladiator*. In the scene depicted, Commodus, the emperor heir apparent, meets with his father, Marcus Aurelius, the stoic philosopher and emperor of Rome, in a tent near the battlefield where the last Germanic stronghold was defeated. Commodus was summoned to the tent by his father. He thought he would be told he will be the next emperor of Rome. Instead he is told he would not be emperor. Instead, the Roman General Maximas was to be the protector of Rome until the republic was reestablished, and the Senate would once again rule Rome.

Commodus, obviously deeply disappointed, says, "You wrote to me once listing the four chief virtues: wisdom, justice, fortitude, and temperance. As I read the list, I knew I had none of them. But I have other virtues, father. Ambition. That can be a virtue when it drives us to excel. Resourcefulness. Courage, perhaps not on the battlefield, but there are many forms of courage. Devotion to my family and to you. But none of my virtues were on your list. Even then it was as if you didn't want me for your son."

In this initial interchange Commodus tries to establish a connection with his father by citing earlier correspondence he had received from him. He emotionally recalls the rejection he felt at the time and the alienation he experienced. He goes on to say, "I searched the faces of the gods for ways to please you, to make you proud. One kind word, one full hug where you pressed me to your chest and held me tight would have been like the sun on my heart for a thousand years. What is it in me you hate so much? All I've ever wanted was to live up to you, Caesar, Father."

You can feel the heartfelt emotion in his voice, can't you? All he ever wanted was affirmation from the one man that mattered the most to him. His father, Marcus, responds, "Your fault as a son is my failure as a father. Come." Marcus seeks to embrace his son. As they embrace Commodus tearfully states, "Father,

3

I would butcher the whole world if you would only have loved me!"

This poignant encounter illustrates the longing of every son and every daughter. We long for a blessing from those whom we hold in high esteem, those whom we love, and those whose regard matters to us. Assuming for a moment that this dialogue or a variation of it were true, how would the course of history have changed had Commodus received the attention of his father he so longed for, felt his embrace, and heard words of affirmation from the one man in his life that really mattered?

Given the events of history—that Commodus was a half-mad emperor who derived pleasure from the death of invalids in the Coliseum at his hand while pretending to be a gladiator himself—would his story be different? This is the same man that fought over one thousand staged fights in arenas, resulting in the brutal death of helpless victims or other gladiators fearful of wounding the emperor. Commodus met his end at the hands of a wrestler who was paid by the Senate to assassinate him when poison failed to do the trick. Had Commodus received the blessing he sought from his father what would his life have looked like? I would suggest history would have recorded a far different story, and his terrible legacy would have been replaced by a much more positive one.

Going back to the retreat setting, once the video clip concluded there was a still hush in the large room of over one hundred men. I ascended the stage and asked, "How many of you have *received* a blessing from your father?" None raised their hands. I asked a second question: "How many of you *longed* for a blessing from your father?" Most men raised their hands. Those who didn't may have grown up in a fatherless home or a home ruled by a tyrant. Yet, I believe that even such men long for a blessing, maybe not from their natural father but from a surrogate father, role model, someone looked up to and admired, a mentor, perhaps, or someone esteemed or highly regarded.

I concluded my message by offering to bless any man longing to be blessed. I would act as their surrogate father on behalf of the heavenly Father if they came forward that evening to receive a blessing. As the gathering broke up after the message, I was asked by a man I brought with me to the retreat, "How many men do you expect will come forward?" I said, "Ten to twelve men." As we reassembled that evening before the message, I repeated my offer. To my astonishment, more than sixty men came forward to receive a blessing. Over the next hour and a half I blessed each man separately. I put my hands on their heads and spoke a blessing into their lives. Many men wept openly. Those observing were visibly moved emotionally.

One man who had received his blessing early on stood close by, observing the blessing of the rest of the men who came forward. When the last man had been blessed and the men were making their way backs to their seats, he came up to me. He said, "I listened to each blessing you gave. Not one of them was the same. I know the life stories of many of these men. You do not. Yet, I was blown away by the specific words you used with each of them. They reflected an intimate knowledge of each man. How did you know what to say?" I responded by saying, "I didn't until I touched them."

This story has been repeated over and over again wherever I talk about the importance of blessing. It doesn't matter in what culture, community, or country a person lives. Every person longs for a blessing. The world can be a cold place, where even in a crowd you feel alone. Every human being wants to know that their life matters and that others recognize they matter. Every human being seeks affirmation, even if it comes from a dysfunctional relationship or place. Everyone wants to be valued by someone they value. Every person wants others to see the good in them, to see a positive future ahead for them, to know that others will help them get there, to have others appreciate their uniqueness, to see potential within them, and to realize the vision for their life seen by someone significant in their life—to see it come true.

## Bible Evidence

The Bible provides ample evidence of the prominence and importance of blessing. "Bless" or "blessing" is found 194 times in the Bible—174 in the Old Testament and 24 in the New

Testament. When "blessed" and "blesses" are added to the list, the total grows to 402 occurrences. Leaders of prominence blessed others of less prominence on behalf of God, the One of Great Prominence. Blessings of this nature were usually administered near the death of the one blessing others. Sometimes blessings were conditional depending on one's obedience. At other times blessings were given in conjunction with the establishment of a covenant or as a reward for obedience. In other instances a blessing was simply bestowed as an act of grace. Even some nations, such as Israel, received a blessing. In some biblical cases a blessing also included a prophetic utterance. Jacob's blessings of his sons carried within the blessing a prediction of their future or the future of generations to come.

Blessings were prominent in the Old Testament. God blessed Abraham and through him the world (Genesis 12:2–3; 22:17). Abraham blessed Isaac (Genesis 17:19, 21) and others of his family (Genesis 17:18, 20), Isaac blessed Jacob and Esau (Genesis 27–28), and Jacob received a blessing from God (Genesis 32:26) and, in turn, blessed his twelve sons (Genesis 48–49). Aaron blessed the Israelites (Numbers 6:23–24), and Moses blessed them as well (Deuteronomy 33:1). Moses blessed Joshua (Deuteronomy 31:7, 14; 32:44; 34:9). God blessed Joshua after the death of Moses (Joshua 1:1–3). Speaking a word of faith, a blessing, on someone is also in the New Testament. Jesus blessed Peter (John 1:42; Luke 22:32) and His disciples (Matthew 28:16–20; Luke 24:46–51; Acts 1:6–8). When Paul is about to be martyred, he pronounces a blessing on his protégé Timothy (2 Timothy 4:1–8).

## Blessing Described

*Nelson's Illustrated Bible Dictionary* defines a blessing as an "act of declaring, or wishing, God's favor and goodness upon others." A blessing not only expresses good intentions, it carries with its words intentionality, purposing, and empowerment now and in the future for the recipient. A blessing implies a knowledge of the one being blessed based on observations over time. Trends, patterns, characteristics, and traits observed are often included in a blessing as is a hope for a preferred future.

*New Unger's Bible Dictionary* suggests "God's blessing is accompanied with that virtue that renders His blessing effectual and which is expressed by it." So blessings often include the bestowing of one or more values that will provide a window through which the blessing is expressed, a filter through which the blessing is processed, and a platform from which a blessing finds its footing.

For instance, when God blessed Joshua after the death of Moses and declared He would be with him, and never leave him or forsake him, he urges Joshua to "be strong and courageous" four times (Joshua 1:1–18). In essence, God told Joshua to live and lead from a foundation of strength and courage. His life was to be marked and empowered by strength and courage. His decisions and actions were to be processed through the filter of these two values.

In summary, blessings are as important today as they were long ago. The rarity of them is sorrowful testimony to an age where its value is dismissed or ignored altogether. Yet, God sees blessing as very important, evidenced by the frequency it is found in scripture. Adding to its importance is the power of blessing seen in the lives of those who have been blessed. Even today when a blessing is given by a parent to a child, a husband to a spouse, a grandparent to a grandchild, a mentor to a mentoree, a disciple to a follower, a teacher to a student, a benefactor to a beneficiary, a boss to an employee, a pastor to a congregant, a friend to a friend, or even a son or daughter to a parent or grandparent, lives are enriched, focus is attained, direction is determined, hope is provided, and value is experienced.

CHAPTER 2

## *The Source of Blessing*

I AM CONTINUALLY amazed by how God uses the people, circumstances, and events of our lives to teach valuable lessons. Through some unfortunate circumstances, our daughter and her three young sons came to live with Debby and me in our home. She was pregnant with our fourth grandson. We believed God was calling us to re-parent our daughter and become surrogate parents to our grandsons. We added twelve hundred square feet to our home to accommodate our extended family. Over a four-year period we strategically invested in their lives, providing for their physical, emotional, intellectual, and spiritual needs.

One evening shortly after the birth of our fourth grandson, Lochlan, my daughter came into the living room and spoke to me. Referring to the fact that Debby and I had lost four babies before she was born and correlating that fact with the birth of her four sons, she said, "Dad, what the locusts have taken, God has restored." What an amazing statement. She was right. God had replaced our loss with four wonderful and precious grandsons.

Debby and I took our temporary role seriously, not knowing how long our daughter and grandsons would be with us. My work with men impressed upon me the importance of being a strategic father—in this case, a strategic grandfather.

We don't have to go far for examples of poor parenting. The Bible is full of stories of poor fathering—Eli, the high priest, and his children; Samuel, the prophet and judge, and his children; David, the king, and his children. In each case, these leaders failed in parenting their children. In some situations they distinguished themselves by serving God faithfully. Yet, they neglected their children. Many people today sacrifice their families on the altar of ministry.

Pick up the newspaper any day of the week, and there are one or more horrific stories of dysfunctional fathering. Statistics abound regarding the consequences of the absence of a father in the home. The National Father Initiative has been collecting data on the consequences of absentee fathers. According to the 2009 US Census Bureau data, over 24 million children live apart from their biological fathers. Children who live absent their biological fathers are, on average, at least two to three times more likely to be poor; to use drugs; to experience educational, health, emotional, and behavioral problems; to be victims of child abuse; and to engage in criminal behavior than their peers who live with their married, biological (or adoptive) parents.

I have a ministry called Heart of a Warrior, which trains men to live lives of integrity, authenticity, courage, and valor. We meet with prisoners at Lino Lakes Correctional Facility in Minnesota every Wednesday evening and have been doing so for four years. Some of the prisoners have taken someone's life, some have been involved in drugs of one sort or another, and most have lived in homes without a father.

In some circles in our society a father is deemed unnecessary. In others, the role of a father is roundly criticized or diminished in importance. But in God's economy, the role of the father is crucial. Engaged and healthy fathers are important to the spiritual, emotional, intellectual, and physical well-being and health of children.

The positive influence of a father in a home cannot be underestimated. This, in no way, diminishes the importance of a mother in the home. Many single and divorced mothers are raising their children without the benefit of a healthy husband or father to share the load. But the role of a father is unique in many ways.

In the book entitled *Why Men Hate Going to Church*, by David

Murrow, the following compelling statistic was cited: "When a mother comes to faith in Christ, the rest of her family follows 17 percent of the time. But when a father comes to faith in Christ, the rest of the family follows 93 percent of the time."[3]

## Three Types of Fathers

There are essentially three types of fathers: the absent father, the emotional father, and the strategic father. The **absent father** may be present physically, but they are absent in every other way. Their routine is predictable. During the week they get up, eat their breakfast, rush off to work, come home in the evening, eat their dinner, watch TV or scope out the Internet, and go to bed. The pattern is repeated throughout the week with some variation on weekends, where they spend their time with friends or occupy themselves with hobbies of interest. Engagement with their children is random and sporadic. They are there but they are not really there. They are often apathetic, self-centered, oblivious to others around them, focused on doing rather than being, and, in the end, detached and unconnected with family. Such men end up lonely and alone wondering what happened to lead them to such a dismal end.

The **emotional father** shows up at the dance recitals or hockey games of their children. Yet, they seem to be more comfortable being a friend to their children. They are often kids themselves in adult clothes. They act like their children and the friends of their children. For a season, a child may think it is pretty cool that his or her dad is just like his or her friends. At some point down the road, when the child has become an adult, he or she will confront their parent. He or she might say something like this: "Dad, when I was younger, I thought it was pretty cool that you acted like my friends, that you were a friend to me like my other friends. But in retrospect, I wish you would have been a father instead of a friend who acted like my other friends." In the end, children need a father.

The **strategic father** is a father who is strategically

---

3 Bob Horner, Ron Ralston, and David Sunde, *Promise Keepers at Work* (Colorado Springs: Focus on the Family, 1996), 111.

engaged with his children. They realize the importance of being both a sage on the stage and a guide by the side. There are moments when lessons need to be taught. And there are times when guidance needs to be given. A sage on the stage makes pronouncements when needed based on his experiences in life. A guide by the side seizes a teachable moment brought on by a situation, circumstance, or event. He provides guidance using the moment as a means to illustrate a value or principle that will help the child navigate their journey of life. The strategic father is observant of what is going on with his children. They are intentional about their parenting. They are proactively engaged. And they are situationally responsive—more about this later in the chapter.

Playing a sport, teaching a course, completing a project—anything worth doing and doing well—requires a strategy. A strategy is a plan, tactic, method, approach, scheme, or stratagem designed to respond to a given situation, event, or a set of circumstances. The word is military in origin and refers to a plan of action designed to achieve a particular goal. So, what does a strategic father look like? What characteristics does he possess? What qualities does he exude?

## Five Qualities of Strategic Fatherhood

In my view, a strategic father possesses five qualities. A strategic father is child-centered, protective, engaged, strategic, and a model to be emulated.

1. **A strategic father is child-centered.** *Train a child in the way he (she) should go, and when he (she) is old he (she) will not turn from it. Proverbs 22:6 NIV*

To be child-centered means that the parent knows the world of their child—their interests, activities, friends, dreams, aspirations, strengths, weaknesses, limitations, and potential. A strategic father understands his child's unique personality, gifts, talents, abilities, aptitudes, and perspectives. They also understand their learning style—whether they are visual, auditory, experiential, or independent learners. Knowing this information will help them "train up their child *in the way he or she should go."* Simply taking an active role of observing a child in multiple settings will give the strategic parent important insight into what makes them tick, what motivates their behavior, what stimulates their engagements, what compels them to act, and what is important to them.

The world is getting darker. Alasdair MacIntyre, renowned moralist and senior research fellow at the University of Notre Dame in Indiana, has stated that we are now living a "New Dark Age." We must do everything we can to help our loved ones navigate the difficult terrain of life by engaging in the calibration of their internal compass so it points to True North, Jesus Christ, so they will not lose their way. It is for these reason I felt I needed to be a "strategic influence" in the lives of my grandchildren.

To that end, I believe God impressed upon me to give values to my grandchildren. A value is a filter through which decisions are processed. A value is a principle to live by. Values help our children navigate an ever darkening world. They provide stability and equilibrium in the midst of instability and unsteadiness as we travel on our personal journeys over ever changing topography.

Through prayer and observation I selected two unique values for each of my grandchildren. To this day, I greet them with their values. At first they were received as terms of endearment. At teachable moments I explained the importance of each value either in response to an event or circumstance. On other occasions I would use biblical stories to illustrate the value. Characters in movies would also supply healthy and unhealthy models for these values. I have even used advertisements to show how companies exploit values to sell their products.

I chose strength and honor for my twelve-year-old hockey player, Braedan. For Kieran, my junior paleontologist, I chose courage and valor. For my budding pastor Gaelan, I selected goodness and integrity. And for my youngest grandson, Lochlan, the comic, I picked truth and wisdom. When our daughter remarried, two more precious grandchildren were added to the family. Derrick, my basketball player, was given the values of peace and justice. Talisa, our dancer, was given love and joy as values. Later on, I will tell you how I came upon these values for each child.

2. **A strategic father is protective.** *If anyone does not provide for his relatives, and especially for his immediate family, he has denied the faith and is worse than an unbeliever.* 1 Timothy 5:8 NIV

Men have been created for three purposes: a cause to die for, a challenge to embrace, and loved ones to protect. Every man I know wants to be a part of something larger than himself—something that matters. Every man I know needs repeated challenges in his life where risk is involved. Every man I know is compelled to protect his loved ones. For the unmarried man, he must protect the unloved, the uncared for, the unwanted, the underrepresented, the marginalized, the widow, the abandoned child. For the married man, he must protect his wife and his children. For every man, any person under unmerited siege, overburdened with the weight of injustice or overwhelming burdens, requires protection and support.

According to scripture, we are to become like Christ, to grow up into Him (Ephesians 4:11–16). Christ had a cause to die for—atonement for the sins of the world. Christ had challenges to embrace—the brutality of the scourge and the pain of crucifixion. And Christ had loved ones to protect—all of humanity, who need the gift of salvation.

There are several areas in the development of a child that require protection: physical needs such as food, water, clothing, and shelter; safety needs such as security, health, and psychological well-being; social needs such as love, affirmation, and acceptance; esteem needs such as personal worth, social recognition, and accomplishment; self-actualization needs such as self-awareness, personal growth, and realization of potential; and spiritual needs such as informed faith, spiritual growth, and relational intimacy with the Trinity. A strategic father also protects his spouse. Children are more secure when they know their father loves, values, and protects their mother.

A strategic father provides a cocoon of protection through unconditional love. This kind of *agape* love is expressed as unconditional regard for the well-being and welfare of another individual through life-giving positive action on their behalf.

Such a love is others-oriented and action-facilitated. Too often a father's love for his children is conditional—"I love you if ...", or "I love you because ...," instead of "I love you regardless." And too often a husband's love for his wife possesses the same conditional qualities (Ephesians 5:25–32). Our children and our wives deserve unconditional love. In fact, God commands us to *unconditionally* love (John 13:34–35).

The scriptural passage that best describes unconditional love is 1 Corinthians 13:4–7. In this passage we see seven things that unconditional love is and eight things it is not. Such love *is* patient, kind, rejoices with the truth, always protects, always trusts, always hopes, and always perseveres. Such love *does not* envy, boast, or delight in evil; it *is not* proud, rude, self-seeking, or easily angered, and it keeps no record of wrongs. In addition to the emotional love we feel for our children, should we not also love them unconditionally?

3. **A strategic father is engaged.** *Fathers, do not exasperate your children; instead,* **bring them up in the training and instruction of the Lord.** *Ephesians 6:4 NIV*

I have heard many parents express the following sentiment: I wish I had been given an instruction manual with the birth of my child. The fact is, we have. The Bible is our manual for parenting—it is living and active, piercing to the division of the soul and spirit, and a discerner of the thoughts and intents of the heart. The Bible is profitable for teaching, rebuke, correction, and training in righteousness (Hebrews 4:12; 1 Timothy 3:16–17). In the Old Testament, God's commands were to be upon our hearts and impressed upon our children. Ongoing conversation regarding them was encouraged during the normal activities of life (Deuteronomy 6:6–9).

I have learned over time that parenting is situational—the style or approach changes in a given situation, set of circumstances, or events encountered along the way.[4] As said earlier, sometimes God calls us to be a *sage on the stage*, while in other situations He calls us to be a *guide by the side*. When should we be a *sage on the stage* and when should we be a *guide*

---

4    Paul Hersey, *The Situational Leader* (Escondido: Center for Leadership Studies, 1992), 71.

*by the side*? It depends on the readiness of those being parented. Readiness is a measure of willingness, ability, and security. The degree to which our children are willing, able, and secure will determine the type of parenting needed to help them become mature and confident in what will be demanded of them as they seek to find their way in the world.

Given the continuum below, a parent should adjust his or her parenting according to the readiness of the child for a given task, circumstance, or event they face during the developmental years of their life.

Sage |----------------------|------------------
----|---------------------| Guide
*Unable and Insecure* (Director)    *Able but Insecure* (Partner)
*Unable but Willing* (Coach)    *Able and Confident* (Mentor)

In a given situation when a child is unable or insecure to do what is needed, the parent should assume the role of **director** and provide specific direction on what should be done, when it should be done, or how it should be done. In this case, direction, guidance, and establishment of standards are needed. As a director, the parent tells the child what is appropriate and how it is to be accomplished.

When the child is unable but willing to try, the parent adjusts their parenting role to **coach**. In this role, explanations are given, specifics are clarified, and persuasion is employed. This the same function a coach provides in sports. A coach doesn't do what is required of the player. Instead he or she sets strategy, encourages players, and motivates performance in accordance with the skill set of their players.

When a child demonstrates that they are able but still insecure, the parent becomes a **partner** who models the appropriate behavior or procedure, provides encouragement as they attempt to do it themselves, and collaborates with the child as they are doing it. In essence, they have moved from a sage on a stage to a guide by the side.

When the child is willing, able, and secure, the parent changes their engagement style to a **mentor**. In this role he or she observes, counsels, and sponsors them as they become adept. A mentor is fully a guide by the side, offering wisdom, insight, advice, suggestions, recommendations, and, on occasion, cautions and warnings.

For example, let's say a child has taken an interest in model plane building. Having never done it before, a father would build one as he or she watched. He would provide step by step directions as *director*. As the child shows a willingness to try to build a model but is still unable to do it on their own, the father would *coach* the child. Once the child showed some ability but still was insecure, the father would assume the role of *partner*, and they would build the model together. Finally, when the child showed they were willing, able, and secure, the father would shift to *mentor* only, offering advice when asked while the child built the model themselves.

4. **A strategic father is strategic.** *Therefore encourage one another and build each other up, just as in fact you are doing. 1 Thessalonians 5:11 NIV*

Bestowing a blessing on your children is strategic because it speaks into their lives value and hope for a positive future. The journey of life—to adulthood—is often a desperate search for a blessing from someone that matters. Every child longs for the blessing of their father (and mother). I have made it my mission to bless my grandchildren. I want them to know that Papa values them, that God values them, and that I see something of value in them.

Several years ago, on my way back from Brazil, I wrote individual blessings for my grandchildren, my daughter, my son-in-law, and my wife. They hang on the wall of the family room in our home and in their home. We call it the wall of champions. Each time our grandchildren visit our home they check the wall to see that they are still there. I bless them every chance I get. Sometimes they come to me and say, "Papa, will you bless me?" At other times, I ask if I can bless them. Repeated blessings of our children or grandchildren over time serve to embed a sense of well-being in them.

*The Blessing*, by John Trent and Gary Smalley, was very helpful to me as I prayerfully thought through each blessing on the long plane ride home from Brazil. I had blessed them in the past with a general blessing applied to all of them. The general blessing went like this, "Heavenly Father, may _____ grow up to be a man (or woman) after your heart. May they live their lives in accordance with the values they have been given. May the life they live bring glory and honor to your name." Later on, I felt led by the Lord to write individual blessings for each of them. I embedded the values I had selected for them earlier in the unique blessing I wrote for each grandchild.

For example, Gaelan's blessing includes his values, my personal observations of him, my hope for his future, a commitment to help him reach that preferred future as much as it is left up to me, and carefully selected scripture that will inform his values specifically and the blessing in general.

*Heavenly Father, may Gaelan grow up to be a man after Your heart. May he live out his values of goodness and integrity in boldness. May his sweet disposition, tenderness, and strength of character keep his feet on the narrow path and provide stability to others. May he have many friends who will enrich his life. May his great work ethic bring him prosperity so he can share with those less fortunate. May his focus, tenacity, and natural goodness make him a mighty warrior for You. May others gain strength from him and be encouraged to reach their full potential because of his example. May he lead others in the path of righteousness. May his beautiful smile warm the hearts of all who come into his presence. May his life be a pleasing act of worship to You. Amen!*

*Psalms 15:1–5: LORD, who may dwell in your sanctuary? Who may live on your holy hill? He whose walk is blameless and who does what is righteous, who speaks the truth from his heart and has no slander on his tongue, who does his neighbor no wrong and casts no slur on his fellowman, who despises a vile man but honors those who fear the LORD, who keeps his oath even when it hurts, who lends his money without usury and does not accept a bribe against the innocent. He who does these things will never be shaken.*

Bestowing a blessing on your loved ones, in this case your children, may be the beginning of changing their futures, restoring your fellowship with them, mending the past where your relationship with them was broken, or finally saying what you have longed to say to them but lacked the courage to do so.

5. **A strategic father is a model.** *For physical training is of some value, but godliness has value for all things, holding promise for both the present life and the life to come. 1 Timothy 4:8 NIV*

The greatest gift you can give your wife and your children is a godly life, a life well-lived. Not a perfect life but a life in the process of becoming yet not having fully arrived; a life of focus, intentionality, and purpose; a life that will bring glory and honor to God, not dishonor and shame.

> *Nobody cares what you have to say until they observe how you live. If you live a life of integrity, honor, and authenticity, people will ultimately want to hear what you have to say—even if they disagree with you.*

Godliness is the sum of Christian values and duties lived out in bold relief—values such as *holiness, goodness, devotion,* and *reverence* to God. The Bible says you have everything you need to live a life of godliness. "His divine power has given us everything we need for life and godliness through our knowledge of him who called us by his own glory and goodness. Through these he has given us his very great and precious promises, so that through them you may participate in the divine nature and escape the corruption in the world caused by evil desires (2 Peter 1:3–4)."

Godliness, however, is more caught than taught. Your children learn more from what you do than what you say. Make no mistake about it; they are watching you. In a video clip titled "I'm Watching You," a small boy around eight or nine years old speaks to his dad.

> *Dad, you don't know it right now, but I'm watching you. Watching the things you do. I'm watching the way*

*you treat people—the way you treat me, my mom, and my sister. The way you are living your life is having a big impact on me. When it is time for me to choose a career and provide for my family, your work ethic will be on my mind. The time you spent with me ... will give me a sense of security. There will be times in my life where I struggle with integrity, and I may not be sure what to do. But I will recall how you stood up for what was right even if you could have looked the other way. And the choices you are making I will also make. Please do not be afraid to show me your failures, to show me your mistakes. I will learn from them. Dad, are you listening? I'm watching, watching to see if you really believe what you say about God. I want you to help show me the way, show me how to live life that isn't safe but is good. So I'm watching you, dad, every day. You're teaching me how to live, whether you know it or not.*

It is true—actions speak louder than words. What message are you sending by the way you live? What message are your children receiving from their observations of your behavior? What kind of lifestyle are you modeling for your loved ones, for those God has placed within your sphere of influence?

All too often what we say bears little resemblance to how we behave. What we proclaim to believe, what we declare we value, bears little correlation with our actions. How we behave, over time, however, reveals what we truly believe and what we truly value. If I were to observe your behavior for some period of time without listening to what you say, I would be able to determine what you really believe at your core and what you truly value. The same holds true for your loved ones. They can see the congruity and incongruity in your life.

They are watching you.

CHAPTER 3
## *The Power of Blessing*

THERE IS POWER in blessing others. When you impart a blessing
you are enriched, as is the one being blessed. Since our Father
in heaven blesses all whom He loves, we bless all whom we love
because He first blessed us. He blessed us with the gift of His
Son Jesus Christ, a sacrifice for our sins to restore our fellowship
with Him. He blesses us with abundant life and adoption as his
sons and daughters. He blesses us with a new heart, in which
resides the seed of the fruit of His Spirit—values from the heart
of God that distinguishes us as members of His family. He blesses
us with new citizenship in His kingdom. He blesses us every
day out of the bounty of His resources. Since He has blessed us,
should we not pass on a blessing to others as an extension of
His blessings?

## A Blessing for My Family

After writing blessings for all of my grandchildren, my
daughter and her husband, and my wife, I looked for a special
occasion to administer the blessings to each of my loved ones
personally. We had planned a family vacation in Wisconsin at the
Green Lake Conference Center. We chose to rent a large home on
the grounds called the White House. As our family converged
for vacation, I saw an opportunity to bestow blessings on my
family. My wife and I chose a balmy evening to gather in the

large living room. We positioned an overstuffed wingback chair near the fireplace.

In succession we called each member of the family, beginning with our grandchildren's parents and down through to the youngest, to sit in the chair while Debby and I laid our hands on each in turn. We then spoke the blessing into each of their lives. It was a very emotional and moving experience for our family. The last to sit in the chair was Lochlan, who was barely able to lift himself into the chair. He clasped his hands tightly, closed his eyes, and told us he was ready. When we finished, he jumped from the chair and hugged us both. Everyone cheered.

As our grandchildren have grown older, they still seek out the blessing they received on the vacation several years ago. Their blessings are now framed and hanging on the wall in our family room and on the wall of the stairway leading to their bedrooms in their home. When they come for a visit I greet each of them with their values, "Strength and honor, Braedan." To which he responds, "Strength and honor, Papa."

As each child makes his or her way to the Wall of Champions, I take the opportunity to ask if I can bless him or her. Most of the time, the answer is yes. Then I embrace each child and read the blessing into his or her life. When they say no, I know it is only a matter of time before they come to me and ask for their blessing. As I embrace my grandchildren and speak the blessing into them, I commit once again to do everything I can, as much as it is left up to me, to see the picture of a preferable future come to reality.

The blessings have produced other benefits. They have served to bind us together as a family, to share a common perspective, to embrace agreed-upon life principles, to provide intentionality and focus, and to set a course for the future, all of which rests on a loving and caring relationship with those who matter in our life—our immediate and extended family. And they have served to link us with the Giver of all blessings—God Himself.

A blessing is a legacy we live and leave in the lives of others. I define legacy as the aroma left in the nostrils of those whom God has brought within our sphere of influence. When God calls you home, the aroma of the blessing you have given others will linger long after and continue to enrich the lives of those you have blessed.

## A Blessing from My Mentor

In 1999 I was attending an invitation-only conference of selected leaders who were gathered to determine how to find and develop leaders for the twenty-first century. Over sixty world-class Christian leaders met over a three-day period. I felt like an eaglet among eagles. In the meetings was a man I had admired for some time, J. Robert Clinton, author, ministry pioneer, leader developer, mentor, researcher, and professor of leadership at Fuller Seminary at the time. I had read most of his materials on leadership and found them insightful, biblically centered, and practical. His book, *The Making of a Leader* (1988), was incredibly helpful for my leadership development.

During the course of the meetings I had the opportunity to meet privately with him. The divine encounter led to a mentoring relationship with him that continues to this day. On numerous occasions Bobby, as he prefers to be called, intersected my life at crucial points offering sound and Christ-centered advice and counsel. His mentorship and research have served to shape my leadership character, competence, and congruence. But I wasn't the only leader he was mentoring.

In August of 2007, approximately thirty leaders assembled in Pasadena, all of whom had long-term relationships with Bobby and into whose lives he had invested himself. I was informed before arriving that Bobby had chosen eleven attendees to bestow upon them a personal blessing. I was among that group. I was honored and humbled. You see, I had given blessings to many men and to my family but I had never received a formal blessing of this magnitude from someone of Bobby's stature and influence. I had given many blessings, but I had not received a blessing from another man.

We met in a large room on a church campus. After brief presentations the blessings began. Each person was called forward and stood with their back to the group but facing Bobby.

There were two components to the blessing, the passing of the baton and the blessing itself. In Bobby's mind he was passing the baton to us much like a relay runner passes the baton to another runner who will run the next leg of the race. He drew this precedent from scripture. Moses passed the baton to Joshua (Deuteronomy 31: 14; 32:44), Jesus did likewise to His disciples (Luke 24:46-51; Acts 1:6-8; Matthew 28:16-20), and Paul did to Timothy (2 Timothy 4:1-8).

In similar fashion Bobby passed on to us, in trust, what he had been given (2 Timothy 2:2) in trust from the Lord. His hope was that we would carry on his mission but in alignment with our unique gifting and calling. When Richard Clinton, his son and pastor of a church plant in Switzerland, was called forward, he was given a tube serving as a baton containing the words Bobby was about to speak into Richard's life. As Bobby placed his hand on his son, he read these words.

> **Baton:** *My passing of the baton to you does not mean I am expecting you to take over anything, but it does symbolize that I honor you as one who can do many things I do very effectively—most of them better than I can do them. It does mean I have confidence in you and that I intend, like Samuel, to be behind the scenes in your ministry always there for you. I will also double my efforts to sponsor you in whatever ways I can. Our ministry times together have always been powerful, and I have learned much from you. Thanks for being a good model. I consider you to be my prime legacy. I know many of my values will live on in you and the many leaders you develop. I also want to affirm your wisdom. Long ago I prayed for that for you, and I have watched you become a James 3:17-18 man of wisdom.*

As we stood to bear witness to this important event, the room was quiet except for the words that were being spoken into Richard's life. You could feel the emotion in the room and the significance of what was being said. These initial comments were followed by the actual blessing.

> **Blessing:** *I fully expect you to move forward*

*following your destiny. You have a rich destiny log. I bless you to fulfill that destiny and minister with power. We desperately need people who can minister with power and model that dynamic to emerging leaders. Wimber did that for you. Pass that heritage on to emerging leaders. I also particularly want to bless your writing efforts. You have a way of saying things "popularly" so that ordinary people can use your ideas. I am claiming 1 Corinthians 15:58 (NLT) as an undergirding life verse for you: So my dear brothers and sisters, be strong and steady, always enthusiastic about the Lord's work, for you know that nothing you do for the Lord is ever useless. I also want to bless your excellent efforts at bringing "wisdom from above" into many situations that need that wisdom. Don't give up on continuing to speak wisdom into those difficult cross-cultural leadership situations you face in post-Christendom Europe.*

We all knew we were part of an inner circle of blessed ones. Watching others being blessed was a blessing in itself. My turn was soon to come. As my name was called, I viscerally felt the importance of the moment. My mentor was about to bestow a blessing on me, something I freely gave to others but up to this point had not received myself. He handed me the baton, put his hand on me, and spoke the following words into my life.

***Baton:*** *Greg, most of our mentoring relationship has been at a distance and involved you using self-discipline and studying my materials on your own, with only minimum feedback from me. You have studied leadership emergence theory, focused lives, and Bible-centered leadership. You have been a good student and have already applied many concepts in your own ministry of high level leadership at seminary level as well as at an "emerging leaders" level—especially businessmen. I want to applaud your warrior breakthrough delivery system. You have used this approach both in the United States and cross-culturally to challenge emerging leaders concerning* *becoming exemplar Fathers and husbands and lay leaders who live lives of integrity that honor the Savior. I also want to affirm your grasp of Bible-centered leadership. You, along with Frank, and Wilmer, and myself have coauthored the leadership commentary on 1, 2 Samuel—including the breakthrough vignette approach. You have set the bar high. You were the first to finish all the assigned material given you from 1, 2 Samuel. Thanks for your diligence. You have a good grasp of leadership paradigms and have identified many leadership insights from the characters you have worked on in 1, 2 Samuel. I am certain that you will embed many of the values learned in your study of leadership into the lives of others. You are a true developer of leaders. My verse for you is Isa. 43:4: Since you are precious and honored in my sight, and because I love you, I will give men in exchange for you, and people in exchange for your life. (NIV)*

These words of recognition and affirmation were like cold, fresh water on parched lips. Receiving this honor from my mentor in the company of others moved me deeply. What followed was even more meaningful to me.

*Blessing: Greg, it is clear to me that God has for you a high-level major role leadership position. Your potential sphere of influence is yet to be tapped at its highest level. I want to bless you with insights into identifying your ultimate contribution set, your ideal major role (specific base and functional components) and then with a major role that will allow them to be put into practice. I want to especially bless you with insights into inspirational leadership. As a high-level leader, you will need to increasingly focus on inspirational leadership. Take this blessing both as an affirmation of what you know already inwardly and as a challenge to see it become explicit.*

It is hard to put into words what I felt at that moment. I was embraced and valued, recognized and appreciated, loved and cared for, esteemed and honored, humbled and moved, and validated and empowered. Bobby's blessing has helped to shape my future. Since that day I have read and reread his blessing. His words speak of an intended future for me, much of which has come to pass while some is yet to come. I have had occasion to talk with Bobby many times in the intervening years. His advice, counsel, and guidance are always in keeping with the words he uttered on the day I received my blessing.

## A Blessing for My Protégé

Drew was a young college student recommended to me for mentoring by mutual friends. By his own recollection he came to me with some fear and trepidation due to the reputation I had as an intense and focused truth teller. Over the next four years we met regularly as I sought to help him become the man I knew he had the potential to be. He listened to my counsel and implemented my advice. He became my spiritual son—a man with whom I am well pleased.

One day recently Drew came to me and asked if I would bless him. When I receive such a request I take it very seriously. I told him I would like to have a little time to pray about a blessing for him. Over the next few weeks the words came into focus. I wanted to select a special place to administer the blessing. I chose the ministry setting in which he and others from my ministry were serving, the Lino Lakes Minnesota Correctional Facility. We had been investing in the lives of offenders for four years. Two journeys are offered—the first helps them tune their internal compass the Bible calls the heart to the heart of God, and the second helps them determine their unique path in the world associated with how God has wired them. They must complete the first journey before they are permitted to take the second.

Drew was not aware that I had chosen a particular Wednesday evening at the prison to bestow his blessing. I felt it was fitting it be given him surrounded by the men he served in phase one. We gathered the men I was working with in phase two with those in phase one. As I walked into Drew's room, he was sitting on a chair on the other side. I asked all gathered to stand as I introduced the importance of a blessing. Drew still didn't have a clue until I called him forward and asked him to kneel—he is much taller than me. I put my hand on his head and spoke the following blessing into his life.

*Heavenly Father, may your servant Drew leverage his giftedness for your glory and honor and your redemptive purposes. May he live in accordance with, in, through, and by the values you have compelled me to assign him—kingdom advance and scriptural authority. May his focused intensity, absolute allegiance to his Commander and King, Jesus Christ, and single-minded devotion to Your cause inform every decision he makes and action he takes. As a fully devoted, disciplined, diligent, and dedicated follower of Your Son, may his life and leadership reflect his commitment to advancing Your kingdom, embracing as his sole authority for faith and practice Your inspired word. May he never flag in zeal or sacrifice his beliefs on the altar of expediency. May he stand in bold relief against the backdrop of his culture, always prepared to give a defense for the hope that is in him. May his life speak louder than his words as a constant testimony to Your faithfulness and power. May others find him strong and courageous while at the same time grace-filled and merciful. May the wounds he endures for Your sake be a living testimony for his unconditional obedience to his calling—a light in the growing darkness, a voice in the expanding wilderness, a captain of his assigned lifeboat pulling others from catastrophe, an ear for Your commands, precepts and values, and a touch of Your gentleness and compassion for the uncared for, unwanted, unloved, and unheard. May he never drop his guard, his shield of faith, or his sword of the Spirit. May he always remember Your divine purposes for his life. May all who know him recognize he is a man after Your heart. And when the race is completed and the last battle has been fought, may he be carried and ushered into Your presence on his shield having given his all and having lived a legacy worth leaving in the lives of all who came with his sphere of influence, left better off than how he found them. May the aroma of his life leave a lingering sweet fragrance that will encourage others to take up the mantle he has laid down. May his life bring glory and honor to Your name. May he finish well. Amen!*

I then read a scriptural passage I had carefully selected to establish, inform, condition, and energize the two values I had given him and that were embedded in the blessing—kingdom advance and scriptural authority.

*You then, my son, be strong in the grace that is in Christ Jesus. And the things you have heard me say in the presence of many witnesses entrust to reliable men who will also be qualified to teach others. Endure hardship with us like a good soldier of Christ Jesus. No one serving as a soldier gets involved in civilian affairs—he wants to please his commanding officer. Similarly, if anyone competes as an athlete, he does not receive the victor's crown unless he competes according to the rules. The hardworking farmer should be the first to receive a share of the crops. Reflect on what I am saying, for the Lord will give you insight into all this (2 Timothy 2:1–7). In fact, everyone who wants to live a godly life in Christ Jesus will be persecuted, while evil men and impostors will go from bad to worse, deceiving and being deceived. But as for you, continue in what you have learned and have become convinced of, because you know those from whom you learned it, and how from infancy you have known the Holy Scriptures, which are able to make you wise for salvation through faith in Christ Jesus. All Scripture is God-breathed and is useful for teaching, rebuking, correcting, and training in righteousness, so that the man of God may be thoroughly equipped for every good work ... for we are God's workmanship, created in Christ Jesus to do good works, which God prepared in advance for us to do (2 Timothy 3:12–17; Ephesians 2:10).*

Not only was I shaking with emotion; he was as well. When the blessing ceremony was completed there was no doubt of the value I placed in him, a picture of the preferred future I saw for him, and my commitment to help him reach that future as much as it is left to me and the resources I have to support and sponsor that future. Actually, as Drew's spiritual father and mentor, I acted as a channel for God's blessing through me to him. Most importantly, I believe he felt God's blessing that evening—I was merely a conduit for what God wanted him to experience. As much as I felt pleasure in giving the blessing, Drew felt God's pleasure as the source of blessing.

There are common elements in the blessings you have just read. Gary Smalley and John Trent have written extensively on the subject of blessing and have conducted workshops and seminars promoting the importance of blessing. They have identified five essential elements of a blessing.[5] These elements include meaningful touch, a spoken message, attaching high value to the one being blessed, picturing a special future for the one being blessed, and an active commitment to fulfilling the blessing. Go back over the blessings above and identify these elements:

- *Meaningful touch*
- *Spoken message*
- *Attaching high value*
- *Picturing a special future*
- *An active commitment*

I am deeply indebted to the important work done by John Trent and Gary Smalley. For years, they have been helping others understand the importance of a blessing and what comprises a blessing. After reading their pioneering work in 1993 and receiving God's prompting over the years, I wrote blessings for my extended family and administered blessings to many people.

---

5    John Trent and Gary Smalley, *The Blessing: Giving the Gift of Unconditional Love and Acceptance* (Nashville: Thomas Nelson, 2004), 30–35.

CHAPTER 4
# *The Essentials of Blessing*

BUILDING ON TRENT and Smalley's framework, I would add three additional essentials: prayerful observations woven into the fabric of the blessing; selection and assignment of one or two core values you hope will become virtues in the person's life; and inclusion of a scriptural passage that establishes, informs, conditions, and energizes the selected values. By no means am I suggesting that John and Gary's framework is inadequate. I am standing on the shoulders of men who I highly regard and respect. I am merely adding enrichments to an already significant, important, and God-honoring structure.

The augmented list of essentials now includes the following components:

- *Prayerful observations*
- *Unique virtues*
- *Informing scripture*
- *Meaningful touch*[6]
- *Spoken message*[7]
- *Attaching high value*[8]
- *Picturing a special future*[9]
- *An active commitment*[10]

---

6    Trent and Smalley, 30.
7    Trent and Smalley, 31–32.
8    Trent and Smalley, 32–33.
9    Trent and Smalley, 33–34.
10   Trent and Smalley, 34–35.

## Prayerful Observations

When considering a blessing for a loved one, protégé, friend, associate, or whomever, prayerful consideration and intentional observation are important. First, seek out the Lord's leading and guidance for inspiration, clarification, and insight. Since the blessing is His to begin with, and you are the conduit of the blessing to another, His counsel is crucial. Ask for enlightenment and guidance. Pray for the one to be blessed. Seek out the leading of the Holy Spirit. Who knows the recipient better than his or her Creator? Prayer should continue until clarity is reached.

For example, I would pray something like this:

*Heavenly Father and Creator, through Your Spirit we gain wisdom and understanding. We are to seek, and the door will be open to us. I now seek such wisdom and understanding for giving a blessing to _____. You know each of us intimately. You superintended our formation in our mother's womb. You knew us before we ever came to be. You have set the numbers of days we will spend on this earth.[11] We are Your workmanship, created in Christ Jesus to do good works, which You have prepared in advance for us to do.[12] That being true, please help me to clarity as to what I am to speak into the life of _____, words that will inspire, affirm, uplift, encourage, give a picture of your preferred future for them that also embraces my hopes and dreams for them—all of which representing who You have wired them to be and what you have called them to do. I will come to Your throne of grace repeatedly until I hear from You what I need to impart. Amen!*

Of course, choose your own words. Again, the purpose of the prayer is to receive spiritual wisdom and clarification as to the substance of a unique and personal blessing for the one whom you will bless. Receiving God's input and approval makes the

---

11    Psalm 139:1–18
12    Ephesians 2:10

blessing all the more powerful and meaningful so the blessing you impart bears His signature.

Second, gather observations gleaned from those who know the person. Add to this your own observations regarding personality, aptitude, gifting, traits, character, skills, plans, dreams, passion, demeanor, mannerisms, deportment, and anything else that will give you a window into who they are, what God intends them to be, and what they aspire to do.

When I wrote blessings for my grandchildren, I took into account certain observed features of their personalities that made them distinct and unique. For instance, Derrick is a friendly soul who values fairness and justice. Braedan is a natural leader with a strong sense of responsibility. Talisa is quiet and brings order out of chaos. Kieran is whimsical and artistic. Gaelan is kind and gentle. Lochlan is very smart and humorous. Their dad is strong and protective. Their mother is nurturing and fiercely protective.

I would recommend keeping a journal and recording your insights, observations, and reflections leading up to the drafting of the blessing. Share them with others who know the one being blessed and add their perceptions to your journal. Answers to your prayers coupled with observations you have gathered will provide the information you need to begin crafting a blessing. Some of the information will be intuitive.

Be careful to include not only your perceptions of who they are but also who you believe they are called to be. Try to stay away from what you want for them, which often has more to do with you than them. We long for the best but often see that "best" from our point of view. Scripture is clear on this matter. *"Train a child in the way he (she) should go,* and when he (she) is old he (she) will not turn from it (Proverbs 22:6)." The message is clear—the way *they* should go is as God has created them, not the way *you* think they should go.

This should go without saying, but avoid all masked criticisms, negative innuendos, and embarrassing remarks. A blessing is meant to convey value, esteem, and regard along with encouragement, validation, and positive perspectives.

## Unique Virtues

A virtue begins as a value that becomes a virtue when that value is acted upon in the same direction for an extended period of time. When it becomes part of one's natural character, it becomes part of the spiritual DNA. One acts on it without thinking. Values are filters through which we process our observations and our decisions. They represent the principles we live by. A value becomes a virtue when it is an ingrained habit. When you select a value for the one being blessed, your hope is that it will become a virtue in their life.

What qualifies as a value? Whatever is true, whatever is noble, whatever is right, whatever is pure, whatever is lovely, whatever is admirable—if anything is excellent or praiseworthy—think about such things (Philippians 4:8).

In the moral sense, a **value** is a quality (such as loyalty, truthfulness, or justice) that human beings esteem and toward which they direct their moral behavior. A value, or values, is a principle or system of principles that guide our moral conduct. Values are the principles we intend to live by—the hills we are prepared to die on. Hunter Lewis, business expert and author, defines values as the personal commitments that propel us to action, to a particular kind of behavior and life. Leith Anderson, Christian leader and pastor, says values explain why we do what we do. They govern our underlying thoughts, attitudes, and decisions that result in behavior.

The fruit of the Spirit is given in seed form at the moment of conversion but requires intentional cultivation before its evidence is visible. I believe the fruit of the Spirit represents the heart of God and identifies the values that should mark the life and behavior of every Christ-follower: love, joy, peace, patience, kindness, goodness, faithfulness, gentleness, and self-control (Galatians 5:22–24).

When values become virtues they represent specific dispositions, skills, or qualities of excellence that together make up a person's character and influence his or her way of life. Plato, the ancient philosopher, stressed four cardinal virtues from which all others find their focus and foundation: prudence (wisdom), fortitude (courage), justice, and temperance (self-control). Augustine, the fourth century theologian, added the Christian virtues of faith, hope, and love.

Peter, the apostle, lists several other Christian values. He urged followers of Christ to "make every effort to add to your faith goodness; and to goodness, knowledge; and to knowledge, self-control; and to self-control, perseverance; and to perseverance, godliness; and to godliness, brotherly kindness; and to brotherly kindness, love. For if you possess these qualities (values) in increasing measure, they will keep you from being ineffective and unproductive in your knowledge of our Lord Jesus Christ (2 Peter 1:5–8)."

The book of Proverbs is full of values God esteems. Foremost, in Solomon's inspired mind, is wisdom. Have you ever wondered why a young man in his late teens and very new to the throne as king of Israel, when given an opportunity to ask God for anything, chose wisdom? The answer is found in Proverbs chapter 4. Solomon gathers his children around him and recounts a story about his youth when his father, King David, spoke similarly to him.

> *Listen, my sons, to a father's instruction; pay attention and gain understanding. I give you sound learning, so do not forsake my teaching. When I was a boy in my father's house, still tender, and an only child of my mother, he taught me and said, "Lay hold of my words with all your heart; keep my commands and you will live. Get wisdom, get understanding; do not forget my words or swerve from them. Do not forsake wisdom, and she will protect you; love her, and she will watch over you. Wisdom is supreme; therefore get wisdom. Though it cost all you have, get understanding. Esteem her, and she will exalt you; embrace her, and she will honor you. She will set a garland of grace on your head and present you with a crown of splendor" (Proverbs 4:1–9).*

His father passed on to Solomon a value for wisdom when he was still a small boy. When King Solomon went to Gibeon to offer sacrifices, the Lord appeared to him in a dream and said, "Ask whatever you want me to give you." Solomon replied, "Wisdom." The seed for this value was planted by his father early on.

The point to remember is that a value doesn't become a virtue until it becomes a habit in your life. When you act on a value regularly, and it is firmly entrenched in your character so that it repeatedly influences your behavior, it is a virtue. Once again, a virtue is a quality of character by which individuals habitually recognize and do the "right" thing.[13]

One day my daughter came to me after I had given values to her four sons at the time. She asked me the following question. "Dad, how did you know to give my sons values that were not observed in their lives but values they needed?" I said, "I didn't know, honey; I simply gave them the values God impressed upon me to give them. I didn't know at the time it was the very values they needed to grow into." How values are selected will be addressed in the next chapter.

## Informing Scripture

What you allow to stand in a privileged vantage point of authority over your beliefs generally and your values specifically matters. What you allow to inform and condition your values will, to a great degree, determine the quality of the behavior it produces. Several philosophies and ideologies come to mind: tradition, heritage, reason, experience, or some other "ism" such as secular humanism.

A secular humanist could have a value for truth informed by his experience or self-interest but the product it produces may or may not be praiseworthy. From his perspective it might be good for business or the esteem of his associates but little else. When a Christian has a value for truth informed by the word of God and held accountable to it the behavior it produces, that will, more than likely, result in God-honoring activity.

Scripture will illuminate the value you have chosen and will inform and condition its outcome provided that the recipient or

---

13 Gregory W. Bourgond, *A Rattling of Sabers: Preparing Your Heart for Life's Battles* (New York: iUniverse, Inc., 2010), 141–166.

beneficiary of the value allows scripture to shape the outworking of the value and enlighten his or her understanding.[14]

For example, my grandson Kieran's values are courage and valor. The scripture I chose to inform and condition these values was Joshua 1:6–9.

> *Be strong and courageous, because you will lead these people to inherit the land I swore to their forefathers to give them. Be strong and very courageous. Be careful to obey all the law my servant Moses gave you; do not turn from it to the right or to the left, that you may be successful wherever you go. Do not let this Book of the Law depart from your mouth; meditate on it day and night, so that you may be careful to do everything written in it. Then you will be prosperous and successful. Have I not commanded you? Be strong and courageous. Do not be terrified; do not be discouraged, for the Lord your God will be with you wherever you go.*

There is merit in blessing your loved ones as a nonbeliever. There is supreme value in blessing your loved ones on a foundation of biblical truth as a believer. Nevertheless, some philosophy or ideology informs your beliefs and values, whether intentional on your part or not. In my view it should be scripture, God's inspired word, truth from the heart of God, our Creator who knows us better than anyone.

Scripture closely aligned with the values you have chosen will serve to frame the future behavior of the one being blessed. The recipient of the blessing must, however, be intentional about allowing the scripture to inform and condition their understanding and outworking of their values. As James, the author of the book of James, said, faith without action is dead (James 2:14–26). For the blessing to be fully realized and the preferred future addressed in the blessing to come to reality, the receiver of the blessing must be proactive and submit himself or herself to its authority and influence.

---

14    Bourgond, 129.

## Meaningful Touch

In patriarchal times, touch was an important element in every blessing. When Jacob, now called Israel, blessed Joseph's sons, he placed his right hand on the head of Ephraim and his left hand on the head of Manasseh. He was intentional about the placement order in this case—the younger with his right hand and the older with his left, opposite of what you would expect. Then he blessed them.

*And Joseph took both of them, Ephraim on his right toward Israel's left hand and Manasseh on his left toward Israel's right hand, and brought them close to him. But Israel reached out his right hand and put it on Ephraim's head, though he was the younger, and crossing his arms, he put his left hand on Manasseh's head, even though Manasseh was the firstborn. Then he blessed Joseph and said, "May the God before whom my fathers Abraham and Isaac walked, the God who has been my shepherd all my life to this day, the Angel who has delivered me from all harm—may he bless these boys. May they be called by my name and the names of my fathers Abraham and Isaac, and may they increase greatly upon the earth." When Joseph saw his father placing his right hand on Ephraim's head he was displeased; so he took hold of his father's hand to move it from Ephraim's head to Manasseh's head. Joseph said to him, "No, my father, this one is the firstborn; put your right hand on his head." But his father refused and said, "I know, my son, I know. He too will become a people, and he too will become great. Nevertheless, his younger brother will be greater than he, and his descendants will become a group of nations." He blessed them that day and said, "In your name will Israel pronounce this blessing: 'May God make you like Ephraim and Manasseh.'" So he put Ephraim ahead of Manasseh (Genesis 48:13–20).*

When Jesus blessed the little children he put His hands on

them. After rebuking His disciples for keeping children from Him, children gathered around Him. He blessed them.

> People were bringing little children to Jesus to have him touch them, but the disciples rebuked them. When Jesus saw this, he was indignant. He said to them, "Let the little children come to me, and do not hinder them, for the kingdom of God belongs to such as these. I tell you the truth, anyone who will not receive the kingdom of God like a little child will never enter it." And he took the children in his arms, put his hands on them and blessed them (Mark 10:13–16).

In an article written by Eugene Harder (2000), he talks about the importance of meaningful touch. He shares the following research that underscores the importance of touch.

> God implanted in our bodies about five million touch receptors. One third of those receptors are located in our hands. Dr. Dolores Krieger, professor of nursing at New York University, found that hemoglobin levels in both people's blood streams rise with the touch of their hands. As the hemoglobin levels increase body tissues receive more oxygen which energizes a person and aids in the regenerative process. Both the (one doing the touching) and the touched receive a physiological benefit. Some studies show that meaningful touch can increase our life span by up to two years. In a study at the UCLA it was found that to maintain emotional and physical health we need eight to ten meaningful touches each day. Drs. Schanberg and Butler at Duke University Medical School found that without maternal touch, rat pups do not produce a type of protein crucial to their growth and the development of major organs was shut down. Put the pups with their mother and production of the enzyme resumed.

When my grandchildren come to visit, I look for every excuse I can just to embrace them, to let them know they are loved and valued. As they burst through the door they run to me for a hug. On occasion I play a game with them. I tell them it is a three-hug day. Over the course of the day I remind them. Or they come in to the house and immediately ask how many hugs today. Some children like to maintain their independence and will refuse a hug—for a while. Sooner or later they make their way to me for a hug.

When adults are considered, we have to be careful that touching doesn't offend them. Touching the opposite sex can easily be misunderstood. In the first case, asking permission would be appropriate. In the second case, if permissible, a side hug would be more acceptable. In any situation, a blessing conferred on another individual should be accompanied by an appropriate touch—a hand on a shoulder, a hand on a head, two hands on each side of the head, or an arm around a shoulder.

Over the course of a visit, my grandchildren will make their way over to the Wall of Champions, where each child's framed blessing resides next to a picture of them. I wait for that moment then ask if I can bless them. Upon hearing a yes—most of the time—I come behind them, embrace them as we both look at the blessing, and I read it into their life. At other times they will come to me and ask for their blessing. The same set of framed blessings appears in their home as a constant reminder of the fact they are loved, valued, and appreciated.

## Spoken Message

Children, and adults, for that matter, value verbal expressions of encouragement, affirmation, appreciation, esteem, respect, and honor—all of which come part and parcel with blessing. These words, spoken out loud, carry significance well beyond what we feel about another but may not say. I cringe when I hear a father or a mother, a son or a daughter, say, "They know how I feel. I don't have to tell them." That simply is not true. When words of approval are said out loud the receiver of those words knows in a much deeper sense the seriousness and importance of them.

Too much of what we feel about our loved ones goes unsaid. When they are no longer with us and we no longer have opportunity to tell them how we feel, we inevitably regret not having done so. How often have you heard from someone, "I wish they were still here so I could tell them ..." When a blessing is given with spoken word, the weight of its meaning and worth is felt by the beneficiary. Coupled with meaningful touch, the experience is unforgettable.

A spoken blessing can be appreciated intellectually, but its import is felt viscerally. When something is felt at an emotional level, it is remembered. As I sit at my desk in the home of C. S. Lewis in Headington, England, writing these words, I am reminded that Lewis died on the same day as the assassination of John Fitzgerald Kennedy, the thirty-fifth president of the United States. I remember exactly where I was when I heard. I was sitting in a high school classroom. I can picture it exactly and remember what the classroom looked like, where I was sitting, and how I felt at that moment the terrible news was delivered over the intercom. Why? Because it was a very emotional moment for me.

When I have blessed others, and I have laid my hands on them, I often feel the person shaking under my hands. They know instinctively the importance of the moment and are emotionally involved in that moment. In this day and age, words of love and affirmation are rarely heard. Left unsaid, a child or adult remains mixed up about how others that matter to them feel about them. Verbalizing a blessing is crucial so there is no doubt about its importance.

## Attaching High Value

The words of a blessing should communicate the value of the person being blessed. These word pictures attribute esteem, honor, regard, repute, affection, favor, approval, admiration, recognition, and acceptance. Braedan's blessing contains within it a recognition of his leadership qualities observed by me over time.

*Heavenly Father, may Braedan grow up to be a man after Your heart. May he live out his values of **strength** and **honor** in boldness. May he never flag in zeal. May the testimony of his life reflect a commitment to* *godliness (Titus 2:11–14). May he never drop his guard, his shield of faith, or his sword of the Spirit. May all who know him count themselves fortunate to be his friend **because he is a friend of Jesus, his Lord and Savior.** May the **"boy of His name"** become the man of His name. May he excel in all he turns his hands to do. **Being by nature a great leader may he lead many to honor You.** May his life be a pleasing act of worship to You. Amen!*

Braedan made a commitment to Christ at an early age. His mother led him to the Lord. I was brought in as the grand inquisitor to determine if the commitment was indeed a real commitment. No one can judge the validity of someone else's conversion other than God. Nevertheless, I was asked to talk with him. I asked him why he chose to give his life to Jesus. He said because it was the right time. He then informed me he kept hearing the same phrase over and over again. Somewhat alarmed, I asked him what he heard. He said, "I was to become a 'boy of His name.'" The somewhat odd phrasing caught my attention. I asked him to repeat what he heard. He repeated it verbatim. I knew at the moment Braedan became a follower of Christ. Conversion experiences are not always accompanied by such a dramatic occurrence, but it was in his case.

In my blessing to him I recognized this moment and gave validity to it by mentioning it. Later in the blessing I also recognized his leadership gift, having seen it demonstrated in numerous settings. These unique sentiments express high value. Assignment of strength and honor as values also expresses high esteem.

## Picturing a Special Future

As Trent and Smalley (2004) point out, "We cannot predict another person's future with biblical accuracy. We can, however, encourage and help them to set meaningful goals. We can also convey to them that the gifts and character traits they have right now are attributes that God can bless and use in the future."[15]

15   Trent and Smalley, 34.

Observations over time can give the blesser a firsthand perspective of the potential of the one being blessed. By watching for indications of strengths and limitations, a picture of a person's potential can be visualized. Strengths can be personality traits, aptitudes, acquired skills, unique gifting, or distinct characteristics seen overtly in their life over time. Limitations are not weaknesses. A limitation might include an absence of aptitude, experience, or training.

Not everyone can be a rocket scientist or a mathematician or a ballet dancer or a music composer. We do a great disservice by creating unreasonable expectations that have little chance of becoming a reality. Trent and Smalley (2004) offer the following caution: "Psychological visualization and picturing grandiose accomplishments in the future will not give a person the blessing. If anything, such practices pile up unattainable expectations that can move the person further away from genuine acceptance."[16]

Kieran is my artistic, imaginative grandson. He has a flair for art and spends hours drawing his favorite creatures. He has amazing rhythm and hears subtle melodies others do not. His blessing contains a picture of a future that includes these characteristics.

*Heavenly Father, may Kieran grow up to be a man after Your heart. May he live out his values of courage and valor in boldness. May he learn to lean into his fear and stand firm for what is right in Your eyes (Ephesians 6:10–16). May his great sense of humor, whimsical personality, and artistic flair* **give him the platform for presenting the Gospel of Jesus Christ to many who need it. May his amazing intellect compel him to articulate the faith in creative, innovative, and compelling ways.** *May he never turn his back to You. May his life be a pleasing act of worship to You. Amen!*

---

16   Trent and Smalley, 34.

## An Active Commitment

This particular element of a blessing has more to do with you than the one being blessed. As much as possible and feasible, it has everything to do with your commitment to help the one being blessed reach the preferred future articulated in the blessing. Implied in a blessing is the responsibility that comes with the blessing. I know that I have a responsibility to help my grandchildren reach their destiny as much as I can in light of my own limitations and resources.

When blessings are given to others we may not see again, we still have a responsibility to pray for its realization. I have blessed many people in my ministry. Most I probably will not see again until we meet in heaven. Yet, I feel the necessity to pray for them. I often include a word of prayer with blessings of this sort and ask for the Holy Spirit's empowerment to bring about the preferred future visualized in the blessing.

When blessings are given to loved ones, we have an obligation to assist them in reaching the future described in the blessing but, again, within legitimate limitations and resources. Such obligation may be met by prayer, frequent words of affirmation, recognition of accomplishments, and verbalized affirmation of observed behaviors reflecting movement toward their preferred or special future. It might also include more concrete examples of support and encouragement such as finances, sponsorship, networking, mentoring, or some other form of tangible nature.

CHAPTER 5

# The Preparation of Blessing

PREPARING A BLESSING is a thoughtful and deliberate process requiring considerable prayer, thought, and reflection. The fact that you are reading this book may indicate a felt need to give a blessing to someone in your life. Perhaps a son or daughter, nephew or niece, brother or sister, father or mother, grandfather or grandmother, or friend or associate comes to mind.

While addressing a men's gathering in Colorado, I introduced the importance of blessing others. In my message I stressed the urgency of blessing people God laid on our hearts. I set aside a time of blessing in the evening because there was such an emotional response to the message. In one particularly moving instance, a man stood and asked if it would be all right if he and his brother blessed their father, who was in the audience. "Of course," I said.

Both men went to the father, who was seated, and asked him to stand. They both laid hands on their father and blessed him. Tears flowed and tender words were expressed. When the blessing was completed, the rest of the men witnessing this marvelous event cheered in appreciation.

Who has God laid on your heart to bless? Just because you may have not received a blessing from your father does not mean you shouldn't bless your son or daughter, or your father for that matter. Many of us carry an emotional wound inflicted on us by our father. Still others have been blessed by a father who loved us and cared for us. You may be mentoring others in your life that would benefit greatly from your blessing.

I urge you to ask God in prayer who you should bless. Who, within your sphere of influence or circle of relationships, would benefit from your blessing, or who longs for your approval and acceptance? You do not have to have experienced a blessing to bless others. How about the forgotten or unwanted in your midst? What about the homeless person you frequently encounter as you hurry from one place to the next? What about children being raised by a single parent or parentless children seeking adoption?

James, the writer of the Bible book bearing his name, addresses the futility of empty religiosity. His emphasis throughout the book is on action that gives evidence of the faith we hold. He says, "If anyone considers himself religious and yet does not keep a tight rein on his tongue, he deceives himself and his religion is worthless. Religion that God our Father accepts as pure and faultless is this: to look after orphans and widows in their distress and to keep oneself from being polluted by the world (James 1:26–27)." Why not be a blessing and give a blessing to orphans and widows?

Although there are many types of blessings, I will address only three: action-oriented blessings, responsive blessings, and strategic blessings. An ***action-oriented blessing*** is one where an act of kindness is initiated on behalf of a person who may or may not be aware of the originator of the blessing. A ***responsive blessing*** is given in response to a particular need or opportunity that presents itself in a given instance. Such encounters are "in the moment," presented by seemingly coincidental circumstances as we go about the normal routines of our life. A ***strategic blessing***, to which most of the content of this book is directed, is one in which we prepare well in advance for someone who has asked for such a blessing or someone God has laid on your heart to formally bless. Such a blessing is a planned event requiring thorough preparation over time.

## Action-Oriented Blessings

Being a blessing is different than giving a blessing. In the first case, action is taken on behalf of a recipient who may or may not know the benefactor. In the second case, a spoken blessing is given to another individual. The words that follow pertain to the first case only.

Giving a gift, paying someone's electric bill, speaking on behalf of and for the benefit of another, providing a service, responding to a need, giving food to the poor, sponsoring a child, underwriting someone's education, visiting the sick and helpless, feeding the elderly, volunteering your services, donating to a worthy cause, or any other selfless act of kindness would be considered an action-oriented blessing.

What we do for others is a blessing. Any act of kindness is a blessing. When an act of kindness is anonymous, it is all the more a blessing. When we serve others and expect nothing in return, it is an act of worship to God which benefits another.

A few years ago, a friend of mine was the main speaker at a conference in Belfast, Ireland, attended by four thousand men. I was invited to attend and conduct one of six workshops offered simultaneously between the messages. Two thousand men came to my workshop, where I spoke about the characteristics of a warrior after God's heart. I presented a challenge to the married men in the arena to outserve their wives and expect nothing in return. I told them to view every act of service as an act of worship to God, regardless of the response of their wives. They weren't doing it for expressions of affirmation or appreciation, just unconditional love embodied in the act of kindness.

Similarly, such acts of kindness are expressions of unconditional regard for the well-being and welfare of another individual regardless of whether they merit such kindness or not. A blessing of this nature, given selflessly and expecting nothing in return, is a pleasing offering to the Lord, which benefits the recipient by meeting a particular need. How can you be such a blessing today? Who has a genuine need you might be able to meet? Who needs a fresh touch from "Papa" through you? Who has a need no one else is meeting for someone within your sphere of influence? Your act of kindness may be a welcome blessing in the difficult circumstances of another person's life and will give testimony to the benevolence of God for His children.

## Responsive Blessings

Blessings can be uttered on the spot by simply voicing words of dedication or approval. I have often been led to bless a baby or small child. After securing permission from a parent, I simply pray a prayer of blessing while gently touching the child. The prayer of blessing might be expressed as follows. "Heavenly Father, I bless this child. Help them to grow in stature and significance. May they become fully devoted followers of Your Son, Jesus. May they reach their divinely ordained potential and become who You created them to be. May they be a blessing to all who come within their sphere of influence. For Your glory and honor I pray this. Amen."

Similar type blessings can be given quite readily when the opportunity presents itself. Tuning your heart to the heart of God in these matters will prepare your awareness of those around you who need a blessing. A simple prayer asking God who you might bless today may open a window of opportunity you could have easily missed if not aware. Some of our greatest opportunities happen at the most inconvenient moments of our lives. In these instances, God does His greatest work through us because we must depend on Him.

We tend to believe God's Spirit moves in what we consider consequential events and circumstances—ones which we have prepared for in advance. Often, however, God's Spirit moves most profoundly in the inconvenient moments of our lives when we are rushing from one appointment to another or from one crisis to the next. Maybe it is a beggar we rush past or a child who has fallen or a person who is weeping or a stranger sitting alone or a foreigner who has lost their way or a friend who is in need of a listening ear—and the opportunities go on.

## Strategic Blessings

Strategic blessings are premeditated, planned, and deliberate. J. Robert Clinton's blessing of me was a strategic blessing. My blessing of Drew, my spiritual son, was a strategic blessing. Blessings for my grandchildren are strategic blessings. A strategic blessing is a gift that keeps giving. Every time it is bestowed, hopefully frequently, it imparts a benediction of approval and impending realization of intended hope. This blessing carries with it informed faith—informed because it is based on prayerful observations, and faith because it represents a surety of what is hoped for and certainty of what we may not yet see.

A blessing is strategic when it has the potential of affecting the course of someone's life, changing direction or pattern of life activities, or opening up unchartered options of significant importance. Such blessings are the result of careful planning borne on the wings of prayer and based on the perceived value of the person to whom the blessing will be given.

When considering bestowing a strategic blessing, the following steps are recommended. These steps are not necessarily in order of priority. In fact, some steps may be accomplished simultaneously, such as observations, interviews, and recording of findings. Prayer may be engaged throughout the process.

1. **Pray often.**

Once a person, or persons, has been identified for a blessing, prayer for discernment, wisdom, insight, and inspiration would be wise. The ministry of the Holy Spirit not only includes convicting the world of sin, righteousness, and judgment but also regenerates, indwells, seals, fills, empowers, leads, and administers spiritual gifts to the believer.[17]

Upon conversion and regeneration, the believer is given the fruit of the Spirit—nine elements: love, joy, peace, patience, kindness, goodness, faithfulness, gentleness, and self-control.[18] The fruit of the Spirit represents the character of God lived out in the life of Christ through the empowerment of the Holy Spirit.

With regard to our subject at hand, the Holy Spirit also

---

17   John 16:8–11; 3:5; Titus 3:5; 1 Corinthians 6:19–20; Ephesians 1:13–14, 5:18; Acts 1:8; Galatians 5:16–18; 1 Corinthians 12:1–11.

18   Galatians 5:22–24.

aids in prayer.[19] He teaches us.[20] Therefore, it would be wise to rely on His guidance in the formulation of a strategic blessing. In particular, when assigning one or more values that will hopefully mature into virtues, the Holy Spirit will help you select the appropriate values.

As you pray, jot down what God is impressing upon you regarding the specifics of a blessing or the components of the blessing. He may want you to highlight certain things. He may indicate a specific future for someone. He might reveal one or more values He wants to shape his or her life, filters through which He wants them to process their decisions or analyze issues or initiatives, or principles He wants them to adhere to.

Pray specifically for the person who will receive the blessing. Ask God to help you determine the uniqueness of the individual, God's design for their life, and God's preferred future for them. Here are some questions you might ask of God.

*What is unique about this person?*
*What are Your preordained plans for him or her?*
*How have you gifted them?*
*What values do You want for them that will mark their life?*
*What statement of value do You want attached to their life?*
*What focus or trajectory do You want their life to take?*
*As I observe their life what should I pay attention to?*

These questions or similar questions will help frame the prayer conversation you have with God. The answers you receive and the clarity by which they come will be from the Holy Spirit. These answers, coupled with gathered observations and interactions with others who know the person to be blessed, will provide the data you need to write the blessing.

2. **Assign values.**

The selection of one or more values is an important step in the development of a strategic blessing. Values are the hills we will to die on, the principles we live by. They comprise our moral system, our morality. It is the filter through which life is

---

19    Romans 8:26–27; Ephesians 2:18, 6:18.
20    1 Corinthians 2:12–13.

processed and decisions are made. Values are what we esteem and find hard to understand why others may not esteem them.

A value becomes a virtue when it is an ingrained habit that one applies without really thinking much about it. Examples of biblically informed values might include centered living, devotion to God, family first, loyalty, justice, mercy, honesty, fairness, hard work, punctuality, self-discipline, courage, submission to the authority of God's word, and being a person of integrity.

Proverbs teaches moral and ethical principles and contains values from the heart of God. The book of Proverbs is an excellent source for selecting biblically informed values. In many cases they are described in contrast to an evil counterpart. I would strongly urge you to read Proverbs and identify the values God esteems as you prayerfully consider what value or values should be selected for the person you have designated to bless.

The primary author of the book is Solomon, third king of Israel and the son of King David. The first nine chapters deal essentially with the value of wisdom. Chapters 10 through 22 represent a collection of single-verse proverbs. Beginning with chapter 22:16 through 24:44 we have sayings called the Words of the Wise. Chapters 25 through 31:9 include wise sayings of Solomon copied from the men of Hezekiah, the words of Agur, and the words of Lemuel.

Chapter 31:10-31 is an often-quoted poem on the virtuous woman.

The value you select may not, in any way, be currently evident in the life of the person to be blessed. What God may impress upon you are values they have to grow into, values to which they must strive to become operational over time. Then again, the value may indeed be evident in their life in some fashion or form.

I am often asked how I chose the values for my grandchildren. At first, there was not a discernable pattern to the process. Some I knew instinctively, but most came after long prayer and discussion with my wife. For instance, Braedan's values of strength and honor were intuitively obvious to me, no doubt prompted by the Holy Spirit, I believe. These values have proven to be effectual in his life. As a strategic grandfather, I have reinforced these values by relating them to experiences he has had over time.

For example, I will recount a story I told in my previous book, *A Rattling of Sabers: Preparing Your Heart for Life's Battles*. When Braedan was younger, I was called to his teacher's office; I thought he had misbehaved. When I got to the school, I was asked to come into her office. I was really worried before she unfolded an amazing story. Braedan is very popular. All the kids love playing with him. While on the playground, he noticed that no one was playing with a certain little girl. Apparently, he stood up before his friends and said he wouldn't play with them unless they played with her. I was so proud.

When we got in the car and he explained what had happened on the playground that day, I said to him, "How does Papa greet you, Braedan?" He responded, "Strength and honor." "And how do you greet Papa?" He said, "Strength and honor." I then said, "What you did on the playground today took strength, and you did the honorable thing." Until that moment our greeting was a familiar and cherished way to connect with one another. Now, however, it took on a very different meaning. To this day, when we are together, he likes to tell me about the honorable things he has done since last we were together.

Although not exhaustive, the following list of values may be helpful in your selection.

| Personal | Spiritual | Relational | Spiritual Fruit |
| --- | --- | --- | --- |
| Decency | Devotion | Compassion | Love |
| Courage | Holiness | Forgiveness | Joy |
| Gratitude | Obedience | Friendliness | Peace |
| Endurance | Prayerfulness | Honesty | Patience |
| Self-discipline | Thankfulness | Justice | Kindness |
| Centeredness | Dedication | Fairness | Goodness |
| Wisdom | Diligence | Selflessness | Faithfulness |
| Strength | Mercy | Equality | Gentleness |
| Perseverance | Grace | Forbearance | Self-control |

| Integrity | Godliness | Loyalty | Poverty |
| Responsibility | Faith | Empathy | Chastity |
| Honor | Hope | Hospitality | Servanthood |
| Commitment | Charity | Caring | Spirituality |
| Valor | Truth | Generosity | Others |

Values can also be expressed as phrases, such as responsibility to family, truth seeker, promise keeper, sacrificial living, others oriented, practical worship, giver of gifts, bestower of blessing, Christ follower, Gospel focused, Kingdom advance, soul saver, life giver, biblical authority, Christ-centered leadership, focused living, people first, being for doing, Kingdom purposes, ministry mindedness, or other such phrases.

The following questions will help in the selection process.
- *What are the things they respect so deeply that they tend to be resentful of those who treat them with disrespect?*
- *What is it that they treasure so highly that they are irritated when other people don't?*
- *What values are currently evident in their life?*
- *What values do you intuitively feel need to mark their life?*
- *What values resonate with your observations of their behavior?*
- *What values describe their character?*
- *What values distinguish them from others?*
- *What values will help them navigate the world ahead of them?*

The objective is to select values that either correlate with God's "wiring" of the person or values you are led to give them which they may have to grow into. Try to avoid giving values you would prefer for yourself or values you believe they need based on some perceived notion of inadequacy or shortcoming. Assigned values are meant to facilitate a person's journey to a preferred or special future. Metaphorically, they are compass points that will help the person find their way as they continue on their personal journey.

3. **Conduct interviews.**

Interviews will help provide objectivity in that you will hear different perspectives from relatives, close friends, and other people who may know them. In the case of a child, interviewing a parent, guardian, or relative would be instructive. The following questions may yield important information.

- *What are your earliest recollections of_____?*
- *What behavioral characteristics make them who they are?*
- *What are their unique interests and preferences?*
- *What are their aptitudes?*
- *What skills do they possess?*
- *What are their dreams and aspirations?*
- *What are their most significant accomplishments?*
- *How do they spend their discretionary time?*
- *How would you describe their personality?*
- *How do they interact around others?*
- *How would you describe their spirituality?*

Any question that can give you clarity as to who they are and what they desire to be will be useful information in the development of a blessing. Of course, your most valuable interview will be with the person who will be blessed. Some variation of the questions mentioned already could be used in this very important interview. If the blessing is to be a surprise, then interviewing the candidate may not be possible.

4. **Gather observations.**

Probably the most useful tool is personal observation. Actually, the questions I posed under *interviews* would be ideal to consider as you observe the person to whom the blessing will be given. You may have the benefit of having observed the person for an extended period of time as I did with my wife, son-in-law, daughter, and grandchildren.

What should you look for? Anything that will give insight into their personality, capacity, character, calling, potential, perspective, uniqueness, skill set, interpersonal dynamics, gifting, abilities, aspirations, accomplishments, strengths, limitations, intentionality, or the like.

Answers to the following questions will help you clarify their personality type. Knowing this information will provide data that can be researched online by simply searching for the type (i.e., INTJ, ESFP, etc.). Understanding their personality temperament is only one piece of the puzzle, but it is a very important one. Our personality temperament is God-given and is an expression of our being.

If the subject is in their late teens or older perhaps you might consider having them take one or more of the following instruments: Keirsey Temperament Sorter (KTS-II), Gallup StrengthsFinder®, spiritual gifts inventory, leadership style inventory, or other related instruments. Some instruments are available online at no charge while others may require a fee.

What have you observed? What do you hear? What do you see? What do you feel intuitively? Do your observations correlate with other information you have gathered? Is there someone you can talk to who could validate your findings? What trends, tendencies, inclinations, biases, predispositions, or patterns have you observed?

Not all of the information you gather will find its way into the text of the blessing. Your observations are simply the data you will consider as you develop the blessing. Keeping a journal to record your findings in one place will make the effort of developing a blessing easier.

# Determining Personality Temperament

**Where, primarily, do you prefer to direct your energy?**
*How do you recharge your batteries?*

| | |
|---|---|
| **E** | People, things, situations, "The Outer World"... Around people. |
| **I** | Ideas, information, explanations, beliefs, "The Inner World"... Away from people. |

**How do you prefer to process information?**
*Do you generally focus on the present or the future?*

| | |
|---|---|
| **S** | Prefer to deal with facts, what you know...(concrete) Focus on the present. |
| **N** | Prefer to deal with ideas, look into the unknown...(abstract) Focus on the future. |

**How do you prefer to make decisions?**
*Where do your decisions come from?*

| | |
|---|---|
| **T** | Primarily on logic and an objective analysis of cause and effect. The head. |
| **F** | Primarily on values and on subjective evaluation of personal concerns. The heart. |

**How do you prefer to organize your life?**
*When considering an issue how do you prefer to respond?*

| | |
|---|---|
| **J** | Prefer plans, stability, and organization. Prefer to have things settled. |
| **P** | Prefer to go with the flow, flexibility, react to situations. Prefer to keep my options open. |

Online Instrument: Keirsey Temperament Sorter (KTS-II) - http://www.keirsey.com/
Our **personality temperament** is our *expression of being*. Our **leadership style** is our *method of influence*.

**Gregory W. Bourgond, DMin, EdD (2010)**

# Prepare a written draft.

Once adequate information has been gathered and you have a sense of leading from the Lord, you are ready to prepare a draft of the blessing. The blessing is a declaration of affirmation, approval, and aspiration for the receiver of the blessing. The essential components of the blessing include an inserted value or values, recognition of their uniqueness, a statement of worth and value, a description of a distinctive future, and a pertinent scriptural passage. Several examples may be helpful at this point.

### Example #1—To a young boy:

*Heavenly Father, I bless _____. May he grow up to be a man after Your heart **(distinctive future)**. May he live out his values of peace and justice in boldness **(inserted values)**. May the tenderness of his heart, the empathy he has for others, and his overt friendliness be recognized as precious and respected qualities **(statement of worth and value)**. May he be a reconciler for the conflicted **(distinctive future)**. May he strive for righteousness **(distinctive future)**. May he be a protector of the unprotected, the underrepresented, the underprivileged, and the defenseless ones **(distinctive future)**. May he serve the unfortunate who come within his sphere of influence **(distinctive future)**. May he always stand up for what is true and right **(distinctive future)**. May his attention to detail **(recognition of uniqueness)** provide help to others in their time of need **(distinctive future)**. May his concern for honesty and fairness **(recognition of uniqueness)** be a source of strength to others **(distinctive future)**. May his life be a pleasing act of worship to You **(distinctive future)**. Amen!*

*Philippians 4:4–8 **(pertinent scriptural passage related to his values of peace and justice)**. Rejoice in the Lord always. I will say it again: Rejoice! Let your gentleness be evident to all. The Lord is near. Do not be anxious about anything, but in everything, by prayer* *and petition, with thanksgiving, present your requests to God. And the peace of God, which transcends all understanding, will guard your hearts and your minds in Christ Jesus. Finally, brothers, whatever is true, whatever is noble, whatever is right, whatever is pure, whatever is lovely, whatever is admirable—if anything is excellent or praiseworthy—think about such things.*

### Example #2—To a young girl:

*Heavenly Father, I bless _____. May she grow up to be a woman after Your heart **(distinctive future)**. May she live out her values of love and joy in boldness **(inserted values)**. Her winning personality, organizational acumen, focus on doing things right and doing the right things, and theatrical presence be appreciated and applauded **(statement of worth and value)**. May she love the unlovable as You love her **(distinctive future)**. May she be a continual joy to all who know her **(distinctive future)**. May her life bring sunshine into the lives of those in despair and who lack hope **(distinctive future)**. May the brightness of her smile **(recognition of uniqueness)** light every room she enters and provide warmth to others **(distinctive future)**. May her sweet personality **(recognition of uniqueness)** win others to Your Son, Jesus Christ, and bring a smile to the faces of those in stress **(distinctive future)**. May she live a full and joy filled life **(distinctive future)**. May she be filled with grace and peace regardless of circumstances **(distinctive future)**. May her life be a pleasing act of worship to You **(distinctive future)**. Amen!*

*1 Corinthians 13:4–8 **(pertinent scriptural passage related to her value of love)**. Love is patient, love is kind. It does not envy, it does not boast, it is not proud. It is not rude, it is not self-seeking, it is not easily angered, it keeps no record of wrongs. Love does not delight in evil but rejoices with the truth. It* *always protects, always trusts, always hopes, always perseveres. Love never fails.*

### Example #3—To a young man:

*Heavenly Father, I bless _____. May he fulfill his designed destiny ordained for him before he ever came to be. May his values of justice and people first **(inserted values)** provide a foundation of service to others **(distinctive future)**. You have distinguished him by a great intellect, uncommon wisdom, deep loyalty, and practical sense **(statement of worth and value)**. His commitment to encourage the discouraged, empower the weak, protect the marginalized, and defend a just cause is admirable **(recognition of uniqueness)**. May his decisions and actions bring glory and honor to Your name **(distinctive future)**. May others be found better off because of his involvement in their lives **(distinctive future)**. May others see Christ in him **(distinctive future)**. And may he finish well, having lived a life of integrity, valor, and significance and left a pleasing aroma in the nostrils of all who have encountered him long after he is gone **(distinctive future)**. Amen.*

*Matthew 5:3–12 **(pertinent scriptural passage related to a concern for and service to others less fortunate)**. Blessed are the poor in spirit, for theirs is the kingdom of heaven. Blessed are those who mourn, for they will be comforted. Blessed are the meek, for they will inherit the earth. Blessed are those who hunger and thirst for righteousness, for they will be filled. Blessed are the merciful, for they will be shown mercy. Blessed are the pure in heart, for they will see God. Blessed are the peacemakers, for they will be called sons of God. Blessed are those who are persecuted because of righteousness, for theirs is the kingdom of heaven. Blessed are you when people insult you, persecute you, and falsely say all kinds of evil against you because of me. Rejoice and be glad,* *because great is your reward in heaven, for in the same way they persecuted the prophets who were before you.*

### Example #4—To a wife:

*Heavenly Father, I bless my wife. May _____ continue to be a woman after Your heart. May she live out her values of devotion and dedication in boldness **(inserted values)**. Her life is distinguished by an unconditional love, unfailing commitment, fierce loyalty, watchful protection, tireless service, and unflinching faith in the face of great adversity **(recognition of uniqueness)**. Her life is a testimony of Your grace and mercy expressed to all who come into her presence **(recognition of uniqueness)**. May she always abide and endure **(inserted values)**. May her unflinching faith and unfailing hopefulness lift others above their circumstances. May the warmth of her love, the enduring gift of her service, and the unrelenting devotion to her family bring Your rich blessings upon her. May her example be duplicated in her loved ones. May all who nestle under her loving, nurturing, and protective wings always give her the respect and honor she is due all the days of her life. She is a wife of noble character. I am blessed because of her. She has always provided the platform I get to dance on. She is more noble and valiant than all of us **(multiple statements of worth and value)**. When You call her home may her memory warm the hearts of all who know and love her **(distinctive future)**. May she be called blessed **(distinctive future)**. May she be praised and held in great honor **(distinctive future)**. She has lived a life worth leaving in the lives of so many **(statement of worth and value)**. She lives up to her namesake, Deborah, in the Bible **(distinctive future)**. Because of her we are better human beings. May her life be a pleasing act of worship to You **(distinctive future)**. Amen!*

*Proverbs 31:10-31 **(pertinent scriptural passage related to her character).** A wife of noble character who can find? She is worth far more than rubies. Her husband has full confidence in her and lacks nothing of value. She brings him good, not harm, all the days of her life. She selects wool and flax and works with eager hands. She is like the merchant ships, bringing her food from afar. She gets up while it is still dark; she provides food for her family and portions for her servant girls. She considers a field and buys it; out of her earnings she plants a vineyard. She sets about her work vigorously; her arms are strong for her tasks. She sees that her trading is profitable, and her lamp does not go out at night. In her hand she holds the distaff and grasps the spindle with her fingers. She opens her arms to the poor and extends her hands to the needy. When it snows, she has no fear for her household; for all of them are clothed in scarlet. She makes coverings for her bed; she is clothed in fine linen and purple. Her husband is respected at the city gate, where he takes his seat among the elders of the land. She makes linen garments and sells them, and supplies the merchants with sashes. She is clothed with strength and dignity; she can laugh at the days to come. She speaks with wisdom, and faithful instruction is on her tongue. She watches over the affairs of her household and does not eat the bread of idleness. Her children arise and call her blessed; her husband also, and he praises her: "Many women do noble things, but you surpass them all." Charm is deceptive, and beauty is fleeting; but a woman who fears the LORD is to be praised. Give her the reward she has earned, and let her works bring her praise at the city gate.*

### Example #5—To a father

*Heavenly Father, I bless my father. Two values mark his life; integrity and responsibility **(inserted values).** I bless him for the model of integrity he has been. I* *bless him for the support he has given me over the years. I bless him because of the work ethic he taught me by example. I bless him because he always saw the best in me. I bless him because he went without so that I could have a future and a hope. And I bless him because he rose above his difficult circumstances, wasn't afraid to admit when he was wrong, overcame his weaknesses, and made something of himself* **(multiple statements of worth and value)**. *I admire his dogged determination, sense of responsibility, and loyalty to his loved ones* **(recognition of uniqueness)**. *I am the person I am today because of the person he was and continues to be* **(recognition of uniqueness)**. *May he finish the race well and bring honor upon His Creator* **(distinctive future)**. *May all who had the privilege to know him count themselves blessed* **(distinctive future)**. *May his example of faithfulness and devotion serve as a model for others long after he leaves this earth* **(distinctive future)**. *May his life be recognized for the value it has brought to many* **(distinctive future)**. *May his life be celebrated on earth as it certainly will be in heaven* **(distinctive future)**. *Amen.*

*Matthew 5:11–16* **(pertinent scriptural passage related to what a life well lived looks like)**.

*Blessed are you when people insult you, persecute you, and falsely say all kinds of evil against you because of me. Rejoice and be glad, because great is your reward in heaven, for in the same way they persecuted the prophets who were before you. You are the salt of the earth. But if the salt loses its saltiness, how can it be made salty again? It is no longer good for anything, except to be thrown out and trampled by men. You are the light of the world. A city on a hill cannot be hidden. Neither do people light a lamp and put it under a bowl. Instead they put it on its stand, and it gives light to everyone in the house. In the same way, let your light shine before men, that they may see your good deeds and praise your Father in heaven.*

**Example #6—To a mother**

*Heavenly Father, I bless my mother. Mother, your life has been dignified by the values you lived out in bold relief: integrity, perseverance, and authenticity **(inserted values)**. You have taught me many things and have imparted values that have helped me **(recognition of uniqueness)**. Tenacity and perseverance are two that have helped me to not give up. Commitment to family is another that gives me the courage to provide a safe environment for extended family. There are others—faith in the face of adversity, strength in the face of trials, belief in myself in the face of doubts, unconditional love for family in the face of disappointment, and dogged determination in the face of discouragement **(multiple statements of worth and value)**. I learned these values by observing and benefitting from your life **(recognition of uniqueness)**. You have been a model for me, Mom **(recognition of uniqueness)**. I am indebted to you **(statement of worth and value)**. When I speak of legacy to others I define it as the sweet aroma left in the lives of others long after we have gone. My life will bear the sweet fragrance of your life and will linger in the lives of countless others because of you **(distinctive future)**. Thank you for your legacy in my life **(statement of worth and value)**. May God richly bless you **(distinctive future)**. May His light shine upon you **(distinctive future)**. When you are called home may the celebration of your life be heard in the hearts of your loved ones **(distinctive future)**. May the rejoicing by those who long to see you again shake the very foundations of the throne of God **(distinctive future)**. May God say to you, "Welcome home, you are a woman after My heart" **(distinctive future)**. Amen.*

*2 Peter 1:3-9 **(pertinent scriptural passage***

*related to many qualities seen in this person's life).*
*His divine power has given us everything we need for*
*life and godliness through our knowledge of him who*
*called us by his own glory and goodness. Through these*
*he has given us his very great and precious promises,*
*so that through them you may participate in the*
*divine nature and escape the corruption in the world*
*caused by evil desires. For this very reason, make every*
*effort to add to your faith goodness; and to goodness,*
*knowledge; and to knowledge, self-control; and to self-*
*control, perseverance; and to perseverance, godliness;*
*and to godliness, brotherly kindness; and to brotherly*
*kindness, love. For if you possess these qualities in*
*increasing measure, they will keep you from being*
*ineffective and unproductive in your knowledge of our*
*Lord Jesus Christ.*

This last blessing is the blessing I wrote for my mother before she passed away. Words fail to express what she meant and continues to mean to me. At her memorial service I shared the following words.

Many children long for a blessing from their parents. My brother, sisters, and I will not be among them because her life was a blessing to us every day. There are five elements to a blessing. The first is meaningful touch (as I leaned over to kiss her forehead for the last time a flood of memories came to mind), her tender kiss on the cheek, her warm embrace, her gentle pat on the back (and sometimes, when we were young, not so gentle on the backside when we misbehaved).

The second is spoken word. She always had a word of encouragement for us; she was fiercely protective of us; she was our greatest cheerleader throughout our lives. She rejoiced in our successes, and she grieved over our disappointments. I loved to hear the sound of her infectious laughter. I will miss the sound of her reassuring and loving voice.

The third is imparting value in the one being blessed. She lived for her children, her grandchildren, and her great-grandchildren. She would brag on us to whoever would listen. She was proud of us. She always believed in us. She possessed a rare type of love for us—the Bible calls it unconditional love. It was patient and kind; it was not self-seeking or easily angered; she kept no record of wrongs; her love always protected, always trusted, always hoped, and always persevered; her love never failed.

The fourth is a picture of a preferable future. Mom always looked to the future, always hoped for the best, always gave the benefit of the doubt, always saw a better future for each of us. She longed to alleviate our pains and our sorrows and replace them with the good she saw in us, to fan into flame the spark of beauty and worth she knew was in us.

The fifth is a commitment to help us realize our potential. Mom always knew our unique potential and spurred us on to reach it. When the world seemed arrayed against us, she would remind us of what we were and the value she saw in us. She showed us how to rise above our circumstances. What she personally experienced in her own life would destroy most people I know. She was a survivor. Her life was a living testimony of her faith in her Lord and in us.

Yes, she blessed us. Now she joins a great host of family and friends who have gone before her—no more pain and suffering, no more regrets, no more sorrows. She leaves behind a great legacy, a sweet aroma, a husband who loved her dearly, sons and daughters who will never forget her, grandchildren and great-grandchildren who will carry on her legacy and her good name.

Mom, you lived a life of integrity, honor, and authenticity. We grieve your loss but celebrate your home going. Heavenly Father, Lord Jesus, Holy Spirit, we commend her soul to you. Thank you for the gift of our mother. May our lives bring honor to her name.

Writing a blessing may appear difficult or time consuming. The reward of bestowing it on someone that matters to you is worth the effort. A blessing is a gift that keeps giving in the life of the receiver, a pleasing aroma that will linger long after you are gone. As giver of a blessing, you will have the comfort knowing that what you have done honors the Lord, gives hope for the future, and will provide a lasting testimony of the value you saw in another human being. You will not be among those who lament what was unsaid and should have been said but now it is too late to be said.

Appendix A provides a worksheet for developing and bestowing a blessing.

5. **Formulate a plan.**

A plan should be devised that addresses specific guidance related to the bestowment of the blessing, including time, location, guests, ceremony, celebration, record, and frequency.

*Time*

When will the blessing be given? There may be a special event already planned to which this special occasion can be added. There may be a special date that means something to the recipient. There may be a particular time of year that would be more appropriate than another. It may be more advantageous to bestow the blessing in the morning, afternoon, or evening, on a weekday or a weekend. It may be fitting to give the blessing on the receiver's birthday or spiritual birthday (the day they received Christ as their Savior and Lord) or some other meaningful occasion.

*Location*

Where will the blessing be given? A particular setting may be more suitable than another. As mentioned earlier, my spiritual son Drew's blessing was administered in prison, the site where we serve inmates and where he is a member of the ministry team. We gave our initial blessings to our grandchildren on a family vacation at a conference center. I have administered blessings in churches and retreats, in my home, in an airport, at a conference, on a beach, and in a lake after a baptism.

Other logistical considerations might include securing permission to use a site, provision of refreshments, invitation of guests, setting up the location, transportation needs, audio/video recording equipment, microphone and amplifier, or any other resources.

*Guests*

Who should be in attendance when the blessing is administered? You may want to invite others to witness the blessing. I would encourage you to ask the recipient if he or she wants anyone to attend the event. The blessing ceremony may be private or public.

If the blessing is given to a child, the attendance of one or both parents is recommended. Extended family may also be invited in addition to friends and significant people in their lives such as a coach, pastor, or mentor.

Make sure the recipient agrees to the guest list or you have reasonable assurance that a particular invited guest would be welcome. The focus of this event is the recipient.

*Ceremony*

How will the blessing be given? You may want to introduce the concept of blessing and its importance just before you bless someone. A brief introduction regarding the history of blessing, its significance, and its purpose would suffice. This should be followed by an explanation of why the recipient was chosen for a blessing.

You may want the person to kneel before you, sit on a chair, stand in front of you, face you, or face in some other direction. You may want to stand next to the person, behind the person, or in front of the person.

When my grandchildren come to visit and they wander close to the "wall of champions," where all their blessings are displayed, I will often bless them as they face the wall. I will embrace them from behind and read the blessing to them as they read it. In prison, I had Drew kneel before me and an assistant stand behind him while holding the blessing as I laid my hands on his head and read it to him.

A brief pray of benediction could conclude the ceremony.

*Celebration*

This is an important moment in the life of the one being blessed and a significant occasion for the witnesses. There should be celebration and rejoicing to mark the moment. Cheering or applause at the end of the ceremony is entirely appropriate. Words of congratulation, affirmation, and approval by guests would be invited and appreciated.

*Record*

What record will be made of the event? In most situations when a strategic blessing is being bestowed, I frame the blessing and give it to the recipient when the ceremony is completed. When I gave blessings to my extended family—wife, son-in-law, daughter, and six grandchildren—my wife included a picture of the person and special matting encased in a beautiful frame. She wrote a blessing for me, and all ten framed blessings reside in our home and a complete set resides in their home. Whether they are here with us or in their own home, they are continually reminded they are loved and valued.

You may want to have the event videotaped as a close friend of mine did with his son. He posted the blessing on YouTube. What makes this blessing so touching and poignant is that little Ian suffered from an incurable illness and went home to be with the Lord not long after he received his blessing. I have no doubt he is a blessing to everyone in heaven right now. His father, Tom, was a strategic father, and both he and his wife wanted to walk Ian home with a blessing before his departure.

*Frequency*

Blessings are bestowed once in the life of the recipient. If it is possible, find opportune moments to give the blessing again, especially in the lives of children. As they grow older, choose appropriate occasions to readminister the blessing—perhaps at a graduation, or significant achievement, a wedding, an anniversary, or possibly after a difficult time of crisis. Perhaps it would be helpful when a broken relationship has been reestablished after a period of discord.

Regardless of the circumstances, you may have only one opportunity—that is OK; make it meaningful and memorable.

CHAPTER 6
## *The Realization of Blessing*

WITH ACTION-ORIENTED OR responsive blessings, there is a good chance you will not see the person again. As their name or situation comes to mind, a prayer offered on their behalf that God would help them realize the full intent of the blessing would be good. Since God was invoked in the blessing to begin with, we can be assured He will see it through to completion. After all, He is the Giver of all blessing.

Every breath we take and every day we live is a blessing from God. His watchful care over our lives, salvation through His Son Jesus Christ, empowerment from the Holy Spirit, citizenship in His kingdom, and a home awaiting us in heaven are wonderful blessings from God. The personality we have, the aptitudes we possess, the talents we enjoy (Psalm 139:13–15), the works He has prepared in advance for us to do (Ephesians 2:10), the number of days we have on earth (Psalm 139:16), and, in Christ, the fact that we are a new creation (2 Corinthians 5:17) are all blessings from God.

## Bringing the Hope to Life

When a strategic blessing is given, it is accompanied by a commitment to help bring the blessing to fulfillment within the limitations and resources you have at hand. There is a responsibility that goes with giving a blessing, especially in the case of a parent. An active commitment to helping someone reach the full intent of the blessing translates the words of a blessing into a confirmation of the blessing.

In scripture, we who have received Jesus Christ as our Lord and Savior have been given a ministry to perform—the ministry of reconciliation. As His representative, we are to be a conduit for His blessing to others. As Christ's ambassadors we are to represent the love of God to His creatures. Bestowing a blessing on others is a powerful way to fulfill our calling. In effect, the responsibility we have in blessing another is to help in whatever way we can to reconcile the beneficiary of the blessing to the scope and intent of that blessing.

> *Therefore, if anyone is in Christ, he is a new creation; the old has gone, the new has come! All this is from God, who reconciled us to himself through Christ and gave us the ministry of reconciliation: that God was reconciling the world to himself in Christ, not counting men's sins against them. And he has committed to us the message of reconciliation. We are therefore Christ's ambassadors, as though God were making his appeal through us. We implore you on Christ's behalf: Be reconciled to God. God made him who had no sin to be sin for us, so that in him we might become the righteousness of God (2 Corinthians 5:17–21).*

Fulfilling our responsibility may include prayer, affirmation, guidance, support, and sponsorship—or anything else that will facilitate the realization of a blessing.

## Prayer

When Debby and I had the privilege of raising our grandchildren for four years before our daughter remarried, we felt led of the Lord to expand our home by putting on a twelve hundred square foot addition to accommodate our extended family. Part of the addition was a family room, a wonderful gathering place for conversation, watching sports, playing games, reading, and all sorts of activities. It is warm and inviting.

The sitting areas along the windows, which cover two entire walls, are actually toy boxes underneath each seat.

## Wall of Champions

Along one of the interior walls rests the framed blessings mentioned earlier. The blessings are a constant reminder of our commitment to our son-in-law, daughter, and grandchildren.

I regularly wander over to the blessings, and as I read them I pray for each loved one that the specifics of the blessing will be realized. Prayer is one way to satisfy the active commitment we have to fulfill the blessing in their lives.

## Affirmation

When the opportunity presents itself, seize the moment to affirm any observed indication that one or more elements of the blessing are materializing in their life. Gaelan, my goodness and integrity boy, is tenderhearted and very sensitive to the sadness or sorrow of others. One day, coming home from school on the bus a friend of his was ridiculed unmercifully by other kids. When Gaelan and his friend departed the bus, the boy, now in tears, sat on the edge of the curb. I was in the garage looking out on the scene. Gaelan sat down beside his friend, put his arm around him, and consoled him.

When Gaelan came inside, I pulled him aside and told him I saw what he did. I reminded him of his blessing and values of goodness and integrity contained in it. I then affirmed him by saying, "What you did for your friend is exactly what your values declare. Your act of kindness was an example of goodness and integrity. You are becoming what your blessing says about you."

Observations of the one to be blessed do not stop once the blessing is given. When possible, watch for evidence that the blessing is being realized. Affirm any indication that it is being fulfilled. Acknowledge what you observe. Affirm what you see. Give voice to what you hear from others about what they have seen in the life of the person you have blessed. Encouragement and confirmation are the oils that will lubricate the working out of the blessing.

## Support

Support can take many forms, not the least of which may be financial in nature. C. S. Lewis gave much of the proceeds of his books to others in need. He supported countless students with tuition. He opened his home to children for extended periods of time during the bombing of London during World War II. He supported many causes that were initiated to take care of the poor. He was a blessing to many, often anonymously.

I am aware of a man and his wife who wrote blessings for their grandchildren. Their dream was to do everything they could to remove any barriers to realizing the intent and focus of the blessings they gave to them. The father of the family barely made enough to make ends meet. When they had little prospect for housing they could afford, the blesser of the grandchildren purchased a house for them. The rent they paid did not cover the monthly mortgage. The difference was made up from the resources of their benefactor.

If financial resources are limited, there are other forms of support. Your presence at important events in their lives sends a powerful message of support. Your acknowledgment of value to others, defending them from slander, recommending them for projects, and being available to them when they struggle are all ways to provide support. Letters, e-mails, and cards are reminders to them of the blessing they have received from you and to which they must attune their lives. A phone call every now and then checking up on them to see how they are doing is another form of support.

You might provide social base support. This type of support refers to the personal living environment out of which the person operates. Over a lifetime, social base profiles and patterns will change. When social base needs are not met, they are "seed plot" for debilitating, destructive, and dysfunctional behavior that will be counterproductive to realizing a blessing. Four areas comprise social base support: emotional support, economic support, strategic support, and social support.

*Emotional support* may include companionship, being a listener, offering recreational outlets, providing empathetic understanding, or affirming personal worth and value.

*Economic support* may include covering living expenses, medical or educational costs, or basic physical needs such as food, clothing, shelter, or transportation.

*Strategic support* might mean occasionally giving meaning to their lives, affirming that what they do is important. Sharing of ministry or career ideas, philosophy, problems and lessons learned from them, or personal development insights are strategic support elements.

Finally, *social support* might include advice or modeling healthy ways to meet the necessities of life, such as diet, sleep, cleanliness, safety, security, or satisfaction of physical drives.

# Guidance

There will be times when the one who was blessed runs into difficulty of one sort or another. They may be struggling with an issue or problem they cannot resolve on their own. They may be headed in a direction that will be terribly destructive. Or they may simply need advice with a decision they are contemplating. Keeping in touch with them will help you become aware of their need for guidance. Offering to help them is in itself a positive and proactive thing to do.

Given their availability and willingness, you might want to consider entering into a mentoring relationship with them. Mentoring is a relational process in which someone who knows something, the mentor, transfers that something (wisdom, advice, information, emotional support, protection, linking to resources, career guidance, status, etc.) to someone else, the protégé, at a sensitive time so that it impacts development or facilitates progress toward the preferred future contained in their blessing. Such a relationship will provide ample opportunities to fulfill your responsibility to facilitate the blessing you gave them. There are many types of mentors: intentional or intensive mentors, occasional mentors, and passive mentors.[21]

An **intentional mentor** is one who helps build foundational truths into the life of a protégé. They may help them establish the basics of their faith, teach them to how to study the Bible, or show them how to share their faith with others. Three types of mentors fall under this category: a discipler, spiritual guide, or coach. A *discipler* assists the protégé in establishing the basics in following Christ. A *spiritual guide*, not to be associated with the New Age movement at all, provides accountability, direction, and insight for questions, commitments, and decisions affecting spirituality and maturity. The *coach* provides motivation, skills, and application needed to meet a task or challenge.

An **occasional mentor** furnishes incidental assistance in addressing a particular problem or issue facing the protégé in which he or she needs help to resolve. Three types of mentors

21  Paul D. Stanley and J. Robert Clinton, *Connecting: The Mentoring Relationships You Need to Succeed* (Colorado Springs: NavPress Publishers, 1992), 35–46.

are associated with this category: counselor, teacher, or sponsor. A *counselor* offers timely advice and correct perspectives on viewing self, others, circumstances, and ministry. A *teacher* shares knowledge and understanding of a particular subject. A *sponsor* delivers career guidance and protection as the protégé moves within an organization or some other structured entity.

You might also introduce the one you have blessed to one or more **passive mentors,** who can provide helpful examples. Three types of such mentors include contemporary, historical, and divine contact. There is a good chance the protégé will never meet these mentors in person. A *contemporary mentor* is a living, personal model for life, ministry, or profession who is not only an example but also inspires emulation. A *historical mentor* represents a past life that teaches dynamic principles and values for life, ministry, and/or profession. Such a mentor encourages ongoing development and presses one to finish well. A *divine contact* may be a person that momentarily enters our life to give us some needed advice or words of wisdom. The import of their words may not be fully appreciated until much later. God will bring the significance of their words to us at a strategic moment in time.

Maybe the best you can do is introduce the person to a mentor they need. Knowing people who can be recommended as mentors is a valuable resource that can be tapped when the need arises.

## Sponsorship

Contrasted with a mentor as sponsor described above, is a more general type of sponsor who may offer sponsorship in a variety of ways. For instance, acting as a sponsor you could provide a reference for employment, a recommendation for school, or a referral for assistance. You might provide an endorsement for them to an interested party seeking a person with their competencies and skills. You might introduce them to your network of contacts and relationships, where ongoing support may be found.

My grandchildren are involved in a variety of activities

designed to help them find their niche. As they mature, I am sure they will move from one activity to the next commensurate with their abilities and gifting. Knowing that such activity is the road to feeling worth and value, working out the values they hold, and reaching the special future you have envisioned in their blessing suggests that your support will be needed and appreciated.

All of my grandchildren are engaged in a diversity of physical activities: basketball, dancing, hockey, amateur paleontology, art, wrestling, and the like. Braedan is my hockey player—a goalie for his team. He loves the sport, and it gives him plenty of opportunities to act on his values of strength and honor. I am his sponsor and have paid for his equipment and summer training. He has become quite good. I only wish he had chosen a less expensive sport or position on the hockey team. Nevertheless, I see this as an occasion to help him become the leader I depicted in his blessing.

Sponsorship may be simply keeping the best interests of the one you have blessed in the front of your mind and seeking times where those interests can be furthered and supported. The point is to be available and willing to take the initiative necessary to expedite their dreams and aspirations in alignment with the specifics of the blessing you gave them.

In summary, as much as it is left to us, an active commitment to helping fulfill a blessing can be accomplished by prayer, affirmation, support, guidance, and sponsorship. Our resources may be limited or logistical proximity might be a challenge. But something can be done within our means and ability to facilitate the values, worth, and special future depicted in a strategic blessing. Doing whatever we can will leave a "pleasing aroma" in the nostrils of those we have blessed, the people who will be blessed by them, and the host of witnesses who will celebrate their exceptional uniqueness long after you have moved off the scene.

# CHAPTER 7
## *The Legacy of Blessing*

THE APOSTLE PAUL'S last letter to his protégé, Timothy, is, for all practical purposes, a final blessing. He essentially begins and concludes his letter with much of what we have been discussing regarding the content and components of a blessing. He relates his observations of Timothy, identifies important values, highlights his distinct uniqueness, and paints a compelling picture of the future for him. There may have been moments of informal or formal blessing prior to this letter. Paul's words here are meant to encourage his protégé on once he has left the world for a better place. Paul lived a legacy worth leaving in the life of his spiritual son (2 Timothy).

Many years ago, the psychoanalytical theorist Erik Erickson introduced the notion of *generativity*. He stated that in our adult years we work to assure the well-being of our children and future generations. Daniel P. McAdams and Regina L. Logan offer the following clarification.[22]

> It (generativity) may be expressed in teaching, mentoring, volunteer work, charitable activities, religious involvements, and political activities. It may be expressed both in the conservation and nurturance of that which people deem to be good in life and in

---

22    Dan P. McAdams and Regina L. Logan, "What is generativity?" in *The Generative Society: Caring for Future Generations*, eds. E. De St. Aubin, D. P. McAdams, and T. Kim (2003), 15–31.

> the transformation of that which people believe to
> be in need of improvement, with the common aim of
> fostering the development and well-being of future
> generations. It is the desire to invest one's substance
> in forms of life and work that will outlive self. At the
> same time, generativity involves the relatively selfless
> nurturance of and caring for the next generation, even
> to the point of giving one's self up for one's children,
> one's community, or one's people.

Highly *generative* people, in particular parents, prioritize certain principles and values and attempt to pass this wisdom on through lessons they have learned on life's journey—expectations they have for their loved ones and aspirations they have for their children, grandchildren, and generations to come.

McAdams and Logan (2003) state that "Erikson conceived of identity as, among other things, a personalized and self-defining configuration of drives, talents, values, and expectations that positions the young adult in historical time and within society. Beginning in late adolescence, the person constructs and internalizes this configuration to provide his or her life with some sense of unity, purpose, and meaning. I may die, but my children will live on. My own story may end, but other stories will follow mine, due in part to my own generative efforts."

So, the desire we have to bless others finds its basis in social research and in the Bible. We long to pass on to others what we have learned. We want to impart something of value to someone God values. A blessing is a means to do so and leaves a legacy we hope will outlive us and be perpetuated in the lives of those who matter to us. Your desire to bless others and to be blessed is a fundamental part of our wiring from the Creator.

If they erect a statue in your honor, it will primarily serve as a perch for pigeons within the first two weeks of its construction. If they name a building after you, chances are people passing by will wonder how much money you had to give for such a distinction. So began my conversations with leading business people a while ago. It got their attention.

These symbols may indeed reflect a life of achievement

or service, but unless lives have been positively influenced what good are they? Many men and women have reached the pinnacle of success evidenced by material wealth, awards, and rewards only to find out their efforts didn't produce anticipated satisfaction. Although the world applauded their accomplishments, something deep inside told them it was a mirage of little lasting substance.

In the movie *Meet Joe Black*, a successful businessman is visited by Death and is confronted with the specter of his own demise in the not-too-distant future. He has spent his life building his business into a highly respected enterprise. An unscrupulous competitor has tendered a tempting offer. He refuses the offer. When asked by his second in command why he turned such a lucrative offer down, he emotionally responds.

"I don't want anybody buying up my life's work, turning it into something that wasn't meant to be. A man wants to leave something behind, the way he made it. He wants it to be run the way he made it, with a sense of honor and dedication to the truth."

The circumstances might be different for many of us, but we all struggle with the desire to "leave something behind," something that will outlive us, something of value for posterity. We spend our lives investing our energy into seemingly worthwhile endeavors, sacrificing everything to reach a perishable goal. Once there, we recognize the satisfaction is fleeting at best. It doesn't bring the joy we thought it would.

So we identify another mountain to climb, much like the explorers of the past. They set their minds on the vision of what may lie behind the next mountain range only to find another mountain. Sadly for many of us, our significant relationships pay the price of our dreams. At the end of our working life, we finally have time to share. But to our discredit, we have few to share with. The field of our relationships is strewn with broken promises, unfulfilled commitments, reshuffled priorities, and abandoned appointments.

There is nothing wrong with striving for success. But if our sense of worth is wrapped up in what we do and not who we are in Christ, or what we can do for others, we can miss the opportunity we have to model the character of Christ in our work setting, community, and family, and in those we hope to bless along the way.

A devotion to one's chosen profession or dedication to becoming successful is commendable. However, when such devotion and dedication become an excuse for neglecting our families and responsibilities to them or our obligation to be light to a lost world, we sacrifice our God-given purposes, talents, and potential on the altar of expediency.

Secondly, attaining success is no guarantee of attaining significance, that elusive state of being we find ourselves seeking when success does not deliver lasting satisfaction. My premise follows. Significance is more important than success. A life of significance is attained by living a legacy worth leaving in the lives of people God places within our sphere of influence. The only legacy worth living is a godly legacy.

Legacy is the aroma left in the nostrils of those God has called you to influence for His name's sake long after you're gone. What aroma will you leave? What will linger in the lives of those who matter to you long after you are gone? What of significance will outlive you when God calls you home? Will anyone be better off because of you? It is never too early or too late to live a legacy worth leaving in the lives of others.

The desire to live and leave a legacy is embedded in us. We are designed for three reasons: a cause to die for, challenges to embrace, and loved ones to protect. Boldly engaging these catalytic drivers in our lives will lead to significance. Living a life of significance leads to leaving a life-giving legacy in the lives of others God brings within your sphere of influence.

Let's look at significance and legacy more closely.

1.  **We are wired to seek significance in our lives.**
Social research indicates that we live our lives on one of three levels. Some live on the survival level with a basic concern for food, clothing, shelter, and physical well-being. Most live on the success level. We have food, clothing, shelter, and relative physical well-being, so we strive to achieve things in our life which will bring us satisfaction. We spend our lives achieving what we perceive is worth achieving. In the eyes of the world

we may be "successful." But living on this level does not give our lives the meaning we seek. Often, we ask ourselves, "Why do I still feel unfulfilled and empty?" It is because success, in itself, never ultimately satisfies us.

These first two levels give us the hope of meaning and satisfaction but always disappoint us over time. The third level, significance, is knowing that my life matters. The most important question in life is, "Why am I here?" The fact is, many successful people feel insignificant and long for significance.

The Bible offers clarity on this issue. Psalm 139 dispels the notion that life happens by chance, that it is unplanned, a matter of fate and circumstance. We are not here by mistake or chance but by decree and deliberate intention.

> For you created my inmost being; you knit me together in my mother's womb. I praise you because I am fearfully and wonderfully made; your works are wonderful, I know that full well. My frame was not hidden from you when I was made in the secret place. When I was woven together in the depths of the earth, your eyes saw my unformed body. All the days ordained for me were written in your book before one of them came to be. How precious to me are your thoughts, O God! How vast is the sum of them! Were I to count them, they would outnumber the grains of sand. When I awake, I am still with you (Psalms 139:13–18).

God knit us together in our mother's womb; He knew us before we ever came to be; He determined the days of our existence.

Secondly, Blaise Pascal, the seventeenth century French mathematician, philosopher, scientist, and inventor, is believed to have said we are born with a "God-shaped void," which compels us to ask fundamental questions about life. The suggestion of a "God-shaped hole" has been attributed to multiple sources. It finds it origin in Blaise Pascal's work *Pensées*, though, interestingly, he never uses those words himself. He says that there is a void within us which only God can fill, although we attempt to fill it with pleasures, sex, and other God-substitutes.[23]

Ecclesiastes 3 brings this idea into biblical focus by informing us that we are born with a sense of the eternal. "He has made everything beautiful in its time. He has also set eternity in the hearts of men; yet they cannot fathom what God has done from beginning to end (Ecclesiastes 3:10–11)."

From this embedded sense of the eternal arises the urge to find answers to three fundamental questions about life having to do with purpose, progress, and permanence. These questions, in some fashion or form, are asked in every culture and in every generation. Why am I here? Where am I going? What is the significance of my life?

## 2. God has a prescription for significance.

First, we have a *destiny* to fulfill—God has plans for us. "For I know the plans I have for you," declares the Lord, "plans to prosper you and not to harm you, plans to give you hope and a future (Jeremiah 29:11)."

Notice the plural—plans? So many of us live in fear of the consequences of bad decisions we have made in our journey. We wonder about that promotion or relocation we accepted. We question the profession we've chosen or the decision we made about downsizing our organization. A million questionable decisions flood the mind. Did we make a mistake? Did we violate

---

23  Pascal appears to be articulating the same ideas that Augustine did in the first few paragraphs of his *Confessions*. Pascal, a famous French mathematician and philosopher, put it like this: "There is a God-shaped vacuum (void, hole) in the heart of every man which cannot be filled by any created thing, but only by God the Creator, made known through Jesus Christ." Although it is not exact, we find a similar remark in *Pensées* X.148: "What else does this craving, and this helplessness, proclaim but that there was once in man [sic] a true happiness, of which all that now remains is the empty print and trace? This he tries in vain to fill with everything around him, seeking in things that are not there the help he cannot find in those that are, though none can help, since this infinite abyss can be filled only with an infinite and immutable object; in other words by God himself [sic]" (Blaise Pascal, *Pensées*, trans. A. J. Krailsheimer [London: Penguin, 1993], 45).

our principles? Did we bring dishonor upon God? Did we choose God's better instead of His best?

The good news is that God is not finished with us yet. He is a God of second, third, fourth—many—chances. The roads we choose in any given instance simply provide a new set of opportunities to live a legacy worth leaving. We may suffer some consequences, but don't be discouraged. God is merciful and full of grace.

Second, we have a *contribution* to make—God has equipped us for His purposes.

"There are different kinds of gifts, but the same Spirit. There are different kinds of service, but the same Lord. There are different kinds of working, but the same God works all of them in all men. Now to each one the manifestation of the Spirit is given for the common good (1 Corinthians 12:4–7)."

As followers of Christ, God has given you and I one or more spiritual gifts to use for His glory, avenues to express those gifts and degrees of effectiveness in the exercise of our gifts—right where you are. There are other pieces to this package including talents, aptitude, skills, temperament, leadership style, maturity, and availability. Together, this package can be used to positively influence others for Christ in our jobs, our communities, our families, and our church. Based on how God has wired you, what can you offer to others of lasting value? Why not a blessing?

Third, we have a *purpose* to accomplish—God has prepared it in advance. "For we are God's workmanship, created in Christ Jesus to do good works, which God prepared in advance for us to do (Ephesians 2:10)."

We each have a purpose to accomplish. We are here for a reason—directly related to our giftedness (spiritual gifts, natural abilities, and acquired skills). You are not here by accident, coincidence, or fate. You are placed here to accomplish God's intended purposes—His redemptive purposes. In response, the Bible insists that God does have a purpose for our lives. We are here for a reason. Our life can count for something of lasting value.

Fourth, we have a *ministry* to complete—our objective is Christlikeness. "It was he who gave some to be apostles, some to be prophets, some to be evangelists, and some to be pastors and teachers, to prepare God's people for works of service, so that the body of Christ may be built up until we all reach unity in the faith and in the knowledge of the Son of God and become mature, attaining to the whole measure of the fullness of Christ. Then we will no longer be infants, tossed back and forth by the waves, and blown here and there by every wind of teaching and by the cunning and craftiness of men in their deceitful scheming. Instead, speaking the truth in love, we will in all things grow up into him who is the Head, that is, Christ. From him the whole body, joined and held together by every supporting ligament, grows and builds itself up in love, as each part does its work (Ephesians 4:11–16)."

In the movie *City Slickers*, the crusty character played by Jack Palance suggests that the solution to the complexity of our lives is focusing on "one thing." Rick Warren, the senior pastor of Saddleback Community Church in Mission Viejo, California, offers this bit of wisdom, "Live for an audience of one." So, what is your primary focus in life? Ephesians 4, verses 13 and 15, gives us our answer—Christlikeness. In other words, whatever we do, wherever we serve, we are to be about the business of producing Christlikeness, first in ourselves and secondly in others within our sphere of influence.

Finally, we have a *legacy* to leave—God wants us to invest in others. "So now I charge you in the sight of all Israel and of the assembly of the Lord, and in the hearing of our God: Be careful to follow all the commands of the Lord your God, that you may possess this good land and pass it on as an inheritance to your descendants forever. And the things you have heard me say in the presence of many witnesses entrust to reliable men who will also be qualified to teach others (1 Chronicles 28:8; 2 Timothy 2:2)."

The following situation bears repeating. Have you ever wondered why Solomon valued wisdom so highly as a young man that when given an opportunity he made it his only request? Where did Solomon learn the value of wisdom? Who instructed him about its importance? We find the answer in Proverbs 4:1–9. His father, King David, instilled the importance of wisdom in the mind of Solomon while still a boy. Later in his life, when given a choice, he chose wisdom.

Every one of us will leave some legacy, but what kind of legacy will we leave? If God takes us home, what will our employees remember about us? What will our families say regarding us? How will our communities describe us? Each of us has something of value to pass on to someone of value. Each of us has been given something of value by God to give to someone he values. When you meet the Lord face to face, will He honor you for wisely investing your talents in the lives of others or will He chastise you as He did the servant who buried his talent in the ground (Matthew 25:14–30)?

3. **Living and leaving a godly legacy brings significance.**

There are four legacies one can live and leave. Live in such a way as to leave no legacy whatsoever. Live in such a way as to leave a bad legacy. Live in such a way as to leave a perishable legacy. Live in such a way as to leave a godly legacy in the lives of others. What legacy will you leave?

Everyone wonders what legacy they will leave. In other words, will our lives count for anything? Will we leave anything of lasting value? Will we finish the race well? Will anyone remember us when we're gone? Will the aroma leave a stench or will it be a pleasing aroma? Will anyone notice we're gone at all? Will we be missed or will others be relieved upon our departure? More importantly, will our lives bring honor to the Lord after we are gone?

I keep a journal for one reason: I want my family in general and my daughter specifically to know my heart. A note to my daughter at the beginning of my journal illustrates my priority on living and leaving a godly legacy.

*Someday this journal will be yours. In it are those things I have received from the Lord. They represent my innermost feelings and thoughts which I hold in high esteem. I leave them to you as a legacy. As you read them know they are the thoughts and beliefs of my heart—those things I believe are of utmost importance for the formation of Christ-like character and behavior. Your birth was the beginning of my life in God. I hope that my life as a whole will have been of some value to you. You always have been, are, and always will be the pride and joy of my life. May God richly bless you. May your memory of me warm your heart during the course of your life. Love, Dad!*

4. **Living and leaving a life of significance requires finishing well.**

I suspect each of you would like to "finish well." Dr. J. Robert Clinton, former professor of leadership at Fuller Seminary, has carefully studied the lives of over thirty-five hundred biblical, historical, and contemporary Christian leaders. Only 30 percent of the leaders in the Bible finished well—these leaders were walking with God at the end of their lives; they contributed to God's purposes at a high level, and they fulfilled what God had for them to do.[24] Of the biblical, historical, and contemporary Christian leaders studied by Clinton, those that have finished well possessed common characteristics.

Based again on extensive study of Christian biblical, historical, and contemporary leaders, Clinton identified six characteristics of those who finish well:

- *They maintain a personal, vital relationship with God right up to the end.*
- *They maintain a learning posture and can learn from a variety of sources.*
- *They evidence Christlikeness in character as seen by the fruit of the Spirit in their lives.*
- *Truth is lived out in their lives so that convictions and promises of God are seen to be real.*
- *They walk with a growing awareness of a sense of destiny and see some or all of it fulfilled.*
- *They leave behind a legacy in distinctive ways—a model life, changed lives, a new work for God, or perhaps a blessing.*

Maybe it's time to get to know those who work for us. Maybe it's time to get rid of activities that have no lasting impact. Maybe it's time to live by the values in which we believe. Maybe it's time

---

24    Richard Clinton and Paul Leavenworth, *Starting Well* (Altadena: Barnabas Publisher, 1994), 13.

to merge our Christian world with our business world, removing the dualism of our existence. Maybe it's time to live our lives for "an audience of One." Maybe it's time to focus more on our relationships in the workplace, in our communities, and in our homes. Maybe it's time to bless those who long to be blessed, should be blessed, or could benefit from being blessed.

## Blessing Loved Ones

Certainly, people who deserve a blessing have come within your sphere of influence. Surely, your family members would benefit from a blessing from you. What legacy will you leave in the lives of those whom God has called you to influence for His redemptive purposes?

Make it your mission to identify loved ones, friends, and associates who could benefit from a strategic blessing of their lives. Live strategically by tuning your heart to the heart of God and seeking those who need a blessing in their lives. Begin with your family and expand out from there. May God inspire you. May you be a blessing to others as long as you live.

# Appendix A
## Bibliography

Bourgond, Gregory W. *A Rattling of Sabers: Preparing Your Heart for Life's Battles.* New York: iUniverse, Inc., 2010.

Clinton, Richard, and Paul Levenworth. *Starting Well: Building a Strong Foundation for a Lifetime of Ministry.* Altadena: Barnabas Publisher, 1998.

Hersey, Paul. *The Situational Leader.* Escondido: Center for Leadership Studies, 1992.

Horner, Bob, Ron Ralston, and David Sunde. *Promise Keepers at Work.* Colorado Springs: Focus on the Family, 1996.

MacIntyre, Alasdair. *After Virtue: A Study in Moral Virtue.* 3rd ed. Notre Dame, IN: Notre Dame Press, 2007.

McAdams, Dan P., and Regina L. Logan. "What is generativity?" E. De St. Aubin, D.P. McAdams, and T. Kim, eds., *The Generative Society*: *Caring for Future Generations*,15–31, Washington, DC, US: American Psychological Association. 2004.

Stanley, Paul D., and J. Robert Clinton. *Connecting: The Mentoring Relationships You Need to Succeed.* Colorado Springs: NavPress Publishers, 1992.

Trent, John, and Gary Smalley. *The Blessing: Giving the Gift of Unconditional Love and Acceptance.* Nashville: Thomas Nelson, 2004.

APPENDIX B

## *The Blessing Worksheet*

**CANDIDATE**

Name:
Relationship:
Gender:
Age:
Address:
Phone:
E-mail:
Why:

_____

_____

**PRAYER**

Impressions:

Insights:

Intuitions:

Inspirations:

## OBSERVATIONS

Character Traits:

Personality Temperament:

Talents & Aptitudes:

Spiritual Gifts:

Competencies & Skills:

Strengths:

Limitations:

Accomplishments:

Potential:

Aspirations & Dreams:

Uniqueness:

Other Observations:

## BLESSING COMPONENTS
ASSIGNED VALUE(S)
Value: _____ Description: _____
Value: _____ Description: _____Value:
_____ Description: _____

UNIQUE AFFIRMATIONS:
_____
_____
_____
_____
_____

DISTINCTIVE FUTURE:
_____
_____
_____
_____
_____

SCRIPTURAL SUPPORT:
_____
_____
_____
_____
_____

## BLESSING DRAFT

Heavenly Father, I bless _____.

Scripture:

# CEREMONY

Time
>    Date:
>    Day of the Week:
>    Time of Day:

Location
>    Site:
>    Floor Plan:
>    Equipment:
>    Refreshments:

Guests:

Ceremony Agenda
>    Introduction:
>    Bestowal:
>    Prayer:

Celebration:

Record
>    Audio:
>    Video:
>    Document:

Frequency:

APPENDIX C

*About the Author*

**GREGORY W. BOURGOND, D.Min., Ed.D.**
President and Founder

## Heart of a Warrior Ministries

www.heartofawarrior.org
E-mail: GWBourgond@aol.com

Dr. Greg Bourgond earned a bachelor's degree in psychology from Chapman University's (1979), a master of divinity degree (M.Div.) from Bethel Seminary in San Diego (1983), a doctor of ministry degree (D.Min.) in church leadership from Bethel (1997), and an Ed.D. in instructional technology and distance education (2001) from Nova Southeastern University. He completed postgraduate studies in the Institute for Educational Management at Harvard Graduate School of Education (2003). He is the author of *A Rattling of Sabers: Preparing Your Heart for Life's Battles*, published in 2010.

His previous experience includes ten years in the defense industry and commercial business and over fourteen years in various ministry positions. He has held positions as a principal analyst and project manager for Analysis & Technology, Inc., senior project engineer for Hughes Aircraft Company, unit training manager for General Electric, and general manager in Burdick Companies. In ministry, he has been a deacon, elder, ministry director, associate pastor, and executive pastor. He completed twenty-nine years of active and reserve duty in enlisted and officer ranks in the US Navy.

He most recently served as assistant to the provost of Bethel University and as director of strategy for online education providing direction for advancement of online education across Bethel University four academic units: College of Arts and Sciences, College of Professional and Adult Studies, Graduate School, and the Seminary. He provided operational support to Bethel Seminary in the areas of distributed learning, budget development, and future strategic operations. He has also served as vice president for operations and strategic initiatives, dean for the Center of Transformational Leadership, and dean of academic affairs and instructional technology at Bethel Seminary with transregional responsibilities in its six teaching locations, four on the Eastern Seaboard, one in San Diego, and the main campus in St. Paul, Minnesota.

Greg serves as a consultant and teacher in the areas of leadership formation and development, spiritual and personal formation, legacy, organizational systems theory and applications, strategic planning, distance learning and technology-mediated course delivery, and small-group dynamics. He is the president and founder of Heart of a Warrior Ministries, a ministry dedicated to helping men live lives of integrity and honor under the authority of God. He has taught many schools, churches, and organizations. Greg has been happily married for forty-two years and enjoys his six grandchildren every chance he gets.

Dr. Bourgond is available for speaking engagements, conducting workshops and seminars, or consulting with churches and ministry organizations. Two weekend seminar/workshops are currently available.

- **Papa's Blessings** *presents a compelling argument for the importance of blessing those who mean the most to us, offers helpful and practical guidance for developing blessings, and provides the opportunity to develop blessings using materials made available to participants. This seminar/workshop is generally conducted on a Saturday at designated locations such as churches or conference settings.*
- **Heart Surgery** *presents the concepts and principles contained in the book* A Rattling of Sabers *to mixed audiences of men and women over a Friday evening and all day Saturday. Participants will be led through a process that will culminate in the development of a personal plan of action to tune their hearts to the heart of God and live their lives with intentionality and focus on what is important from God's perspective.*

If your church or ministry organization would like more information regarding these seminar/workshops or is interested in hosting either of them, please contact Heart of a Warrior Ministries at HOAWAdvance@aol.com or contact the author directly at Bourgond@aol.com.

*Previous Work*

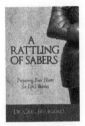

*A Rattling of Sabers: Preparing Your Heart for Life's Battles*
By Dr. Greg Bourgond

In *A Rattling of Sabers: Preparing Your Heart for Life's Battles,*
a Christian minister leads men on a spiritual journey that will
help them embrace a renewed relationship with Christ and a life
filled with integrity, authenticity, courage, and honor under the
authority of God.

Dr. Bourgond, president and founder of Heart of a Warrior
Ministries, has dedicated nearly four decades to ministering to
men through discipleship, mentoring, teaching, and leadership
development. While guiding men on a journey to wholeness by
helping them calibrate their own hearts to the heart of God,
Dr. Bourgond shares life illustrations and fresh theological
insights that will teach men to live a godly life—one that will
bring glory and honor to God, provide an example of a life well

lived, and positively impact all who come within their sphere of influence.

Dr. Bourgond identifies situational lifestyles that men adopt to navigate the pathways of our lives, presents God's preferred lifestyle as an alternative, addresses the real battlefield for change and transformation that will help men reach the objectives of God's preferred lifestyle, offers guidance on how to correct corrupted behavior by addressing the underlying catalysts for such behavior, how to employ lasting removal and replacement of these influences, and how to prescribe a journey that will help a man proactively live a godly life designed to finish well.

*A Rattling of Sabers* offers a process that will calibrate your internal compass the Bible calls the heart so that it will accurately point the way to a truly transformed life—one that will leave a pleasing aroma in the lives of others long after we are called to our eternal home.

This book is available in three formats—hardcover, softcover, and e-book—and can be purchased at Amazon.com, Barnes and Noble.com, or iUniverse.

Along with this resource, additional materials can be purchased to lead small groups on a journey that will help men live lives of integrity, authenticity, and honor—to be what God intended them to be all along.

- *A video series provides an orientation to the journey that will tune each man's heart to the heart of God. The video series also presents an introduction to each lesson in an accompanying manual. One video set per group is recommended.*
- *The journey manual contains twelve lessons designed to help men calibrate their internal compass, the heart, so it points to True North, Jesus Christ. A calibrated heart is necessary to navigate the journey called life. Each member of a small group should have a manual.*

If you are interested in hearing more about these groups or leading such a group, please contact Heart of a Warrior Ministries at HOAWAdvance@aol.com. The video set and manuals can be purchased at www.heartofawarrior.org.